eg:

core ideals =
respect for persons

liberty: autonomy
privacy
self-development

• incompatible w/ many
doctrines of individualism

INDIVIDUALISM

KEY CONCEPTS
IN THE SOCIAL SCIENCES

GENERAL EDITORS

PHILIP RIEFF
Benjamin Franklin Professor of Sociology
University of Pennsylvania

BRYAN R. WILSON
Reader in Sociology, University of Oxford
Fellow of All Souls College

Also in this series:

RATIONALITY
Edited by Bryan R. Wilson

SOCIAL CHANGE
Edited by Robert Nisbet

Forthcoming:

REVOLUTION
Jean Baechler

IDEOLOGY
Lewis Feuer

SEXUALITY
Helmut Schelsky

KEY CONCEPTS
IN THE SOCIAL SCIENCES

INDIVIDUALISM

STEVEN LUKES

OXFORD · BASIL BLACKWELL

ISBN 0 631 14750 0 (cased edition)

Printed in Great Britain by
Western Printing Services Ltd, Bristol
and bound at the Kemp Hall Bindery, Oxford

To my Parents

Contents

PART THREE: THE RELATIONS BETWEEN
THESE IDEAS

Foreword

'Individualism' is a word that has come to be used with an unusual lack of precision. Consider the following passage from Élie Halévy's *The Growth of Philosophic Radicalism*:

In the whole of modern Europe it is a fact that individuals have assumed consciousness of their autonomy, and that every one demands the respect of all the others, whom he considers as his fellows, or equals: society appears, and perhaps appears more and more, as issuing from the considered will of the individuals which make it up. The very appearance and success of individualistic doctrines would alone be enough to prove that, in western society, individualism is the true philosophy. Individualism is the common characteristic of Roman law and Christian morality. It is individualism which creates the likeness between the philosophies, in other respects so different, of Rousseau, Kant, and Bentham. Even today it is permissible to plead the cause of individualism, whether it be considered as a method of explaining social facts, or as a practical doctrine, capable of determining the direction of the reformer's activity.[1]

As we shall see, this passage encompasses a good proportion of the distinct elements typically combined by the term. What it says is, as it stands, both confused and confusing. It slides from individual autonomy to equality of respect to the idea that society is the product of individual wills; from Roman

[1] É. Halévy, *The Growth of Philosophic Radicalism* (1901–4), tr. M. Morris, new ed., London, 1934, p. 504.

law to Christian morality; from Rousseau and Kant to Bentham; and from a methodological to a practical doctrine. The term 'individualism' gives all this an illusory air of unity and coherence.

The aim of this short book is threefold: in the first Part, to survey the range of meanings the term has carried in western thought; in the second, to isolate some of the distinct unit-ideas (and intellectual traditions) which the use of the word has come to conflate—unit-ideas whose logical and conceptual relations to one another are by no means clear; and in the third, to explore those relations and seek to show which elements of individualism hang together and which do not.

Though I have mulled over these issues for a number of years, the conclusions I reach in Part Three were written at some speed, and with the conscious intention of getting somewhere fast, rather than being distracted by the treacherous complexities underfoot. For pointing many of these out to me, while reassuring me that the journey was worthwhile, I am very grateful to my colleague and friend Bill Weinstein. For their valuable comments on my manuscript, I must also thank Anthony Arblaster, G. A. Cohen, Alan Montefiore, Derek Parfit, Carole Pateman and Philip Rieff. In addition I am grateful to all those who discussed these ideas with me when they were presented in lectures at Oxford, and especially to Charles J. McCracken. My thanks are also due to Guy Parkhurst for help with the bibliography, and to Deborah Thompson for preparing the index.

Earlier versions of some of the material in the first two Parts of this book have appeared in the form of three articles by the author: 'The Meanings of "Individualism"', *Journal of the History of Ideas*, XXXII (1971), pp. 45–66; 'Methodological Individualism Reconsidered', *British Journal of Sociology*, XIX (1968), pp. 119–29; and 'Individualism' in *Dictionary of the History of Ideas*, ed. P. P. Wiener, New York, 1973.

PART ONE

The Semantic History of 'Individualism'

We shall begin with the fact that the same word, or the same
concept in most cases, means very different things when used by
differently situated persons.

KARL MANNHEIM[1]

'Individualism', like 'socialism' and 'communism', is a nineteenth-century word. In seeking to identify its various distinct
traditions of use, I shall concentrate on its nineteenth-century
history, for this is what chiefly determined its twentieth-
century meanings. Obviously, given limitations of space, my
method must be impressionistic. The main purpose here is to
indicate both the variety and the directions of the main paths
traced during the term's rich semantic history. The interest of
such an account is, however, neither merely semantic nor
merely historical. The meanings of words generally incap-
sulate ideas, even theories. Consequently, where semantic
divergences systematically follow social and cultural (in this
case primarily national) lines, to explain those divergences
becomes a challenging problem in the sociology of knowledge.

[1] K. Mannheim, *Ideology and Utopia* (paperback ed.), London, 1960, p.
245. In what follows I am particularly indebted to the studies by Koebner,
Swart and Arieli, cited below.

CHAPTER 1

France

The first uses of the term, in its French form *'individualisme'*, grew out of the general European reaction to the French Revolution and to its alleged source, the thought of the Enlightenment.[1] Conservative thought in the early nineteenth century was virtually unanimous in condemning the appeal to the reason, interests and rights of the individual; as Burke had said: 'Individuals pass like shadows; but the commonwealth is fixed and stable.'[2] The Revolution was proof that ideas exalting the individual imperilled the stability of the commonwealth, dissolving it into 'an unsocial, uncivil, unconnected chaos of elementary principles'.[3] Conservative thinkers, above all in France and Germany, shared Burke's scorn for the individual's 'private stock of reason' and his fear lest 'the commonwealth itself would, in a few generations, crumble away, be disconnected into the dust and powder of individuality, and at length dispersed to all the winds of heaven', as well as his

[1] *See* H. Peyre, 'The Influence of Eighteenth Century Ideas on the French Revolution', *Journal of the History of Ideas*, X (1949), pp. 63–87 and W. F. Church (ed.), *The Influence of the Enlightenment on the French Revolution*, Boston, 1964.

[2] 'Speech on the Economic Reform' (1780) in *Works* (The World's Classics), London, 1906, Vol. II, p. 357.

[3] *Reflections on the Revolution in France* (1790), (Everyman's Library), London, 1910, p. 94.

certainty that 'Society requires' that 'the inclinations of men should frequently be thwarted, their will controlled, and their passions brought into subjection'.[4]

These sentiments were found at their most extreme among the Catholic restorationist thinkers in France. According to Joseph de Maistre, the social order had been 'shattered to its foundations because there was too much liberty in Europe and not enough Religion'; everywhere authority was weakening and there was a frightening growth of 'individual opinion [*l'esprit particulier*]'.[5] The individual's reason was 'of its nature the mortal enemy of all association': its exercise spelt spiritual and civil anarchy. Infallibility was an essential condition of the maintenance of society, and indeed government was 'a true religion', with 'its dogmas, its mysteries, its priests; to submit it to individual discussion is to destroy it'.[6] In the earliest known use of the word, de Maistre spoke in 1820 of 'this deep and frightening division of minds, this infinite fragmentation of all doctrines, political protestantism carried to the most absolute individualism'.[7]

[4] *Ibid.*, pp. 84, 93, 57. *See* D. Bagge, *Les Idées politiques en France sous la Restauration*, Paris, 1952 and K. Mannheim, 'Conservative Thought', in *Essays in Sociology and Social Psychology*, London, 1953.

[5] J. de Maistre, *Du Pape* (1821), bk. III, ch. II in *Oeuvres complètes*, Lyon, 1884-7, Vol. II, pp. 342, 346.

[6] J. de Maistre, *Étude sur la souveraineté* (1884), Bk. I, Ch. X in *Oeuvres complètes*, Vol. I, pp. 375-6.

[7] 'Extrait d'une conversation' in *Oeuvres complètes*, Vol. XIV, p. 286. Compare, however, the words of Bishop Bossuet one and a half centuries earlier at the funeral of Henriette-Marie, widow of Charles I of England, in 1669:

Everyman . . . constituted himself a tribunal wherein he was the arbiter of his own belief. . . . Hence it was very predictable that, there being no further limit upon licence, sects would infinitely multiply, and stubbornness would be invincible. . . . God, in order to punish the irreligious waverings of these folk, abandoned them to the intemperance of their mad curiosity. . . . It is not at all astonishing that they thereupon lost

These counter-revolutionary thinkers agreed in giving to 'society' the same exclusive emphasis that they accused the eighteenth-century *philosophes* of giving to 'the individual'. Society for de Maistre was God-given and natural, and he wished the individual's mind to lose itself in that of the nation 'as a river which flows into the ocean still exists in the mass of the water, but without name and distinct reality';[8] while for de Bonald 'man only exists for society and society only educates him for itself'.[9] The ideas of the *philosophes* were, they thought, not merely false; they were wicked and dangerous. According to Lamennais, they proclaimed the individual as sovereign over himself in the most absolute sense:

His reason—that is his law, his truth, his justice. To seek to impose on him an obligation he has not previously imposed on himself by his own thought and will is to violate the most sacred of his rights. . . . Hence, no legislation, no power is possible, and the same doctrine which produces anarchy in men's minds further produces an irremediable political anarchy, and overturns the very bases of human society.

Were such principles to prevail, 'what could one foresee but troubles, disorders, calamities without end and universal dissolution?' Man, Lamennais argued, 'lives only in society' and 'institutions, laws, governments draw all their strength

---

respect for majesty and for the laws, nor that they became factious, rebellious and intransigent. You unnerve religion when you meddle with it, when you deprive it of a certain gravity which alone can hold populations in check.

(cited in B. Dunham, *Heroes and Heretics*, New York, 1964, p. 308. I am grateful to Prof. T. Verhave for drawing my attention to this striking foreshadowing of de Maistre).

[8] *Étude sur la souveraineté* (1884), Bk. I, Ch. X in *Oeuvres complètes*, Vol. I, p. 376.

[9] L. de Bonald, *Théorie du pouvoir* (1796), Préface in *Oeuvres*, Paris, 1854, Vol. I, p. 103.

from a certain concourse of thoughts and wills'. 'What', he asked, 'is power without obedience? What is law without duty?' and he answered:

Individualism which destroys the very idea of obedience and of duty, thereby destroying both power and law; and what then remains but a terrifying confusion of interests, passions and diverse opinions?[10]

It was the disciples of Claude Henri de Saint-Simon,[11] who were the first to use '*individualisme*' systematically, in the mid-1820's.[12] Saint-Simonism shared the ideas of the counter-revolutionaries—their critique of the Enlightenment's glorification of the individual, their horror of social atomization and anarchy, as well as their desire for an organic, stable, hierarchically organized, harmonious social order. But it applied these ideas in a historically progressive direction: that social order was not to be the ecclesiastical and feudal order of the past, but the industrial order of the future (with a large cadre of welfare workers to better the lot of the less favoured). Indeed, the proselytizing Saint-Simonians systematized their master's ideas into an activist and extremely influential secular religion, an ideological force which served as a Protestant ethic for the expanding capitalism of the Catholic countries in nineteenth-century Europe.

History for the Saint-Simonians was a cycle of 'critical' and 'organic' periods. The former were 'filled with disorder; they destroy former social relations, and everywhere tend towards egoism'; the latter were unified, organized and stable (the previous instances in Europe being the ancient polytheistic

[10] F. de Lamennais, *Des Progrès de la révolution et de la guerre contre l'église* (1829), Ch. I in *Oeuvres complètes*, Paris, 1836–7, Vol. IX, pp. 17–18.

[11] *See* the author's chapter on Saint-Simon in T. Raison (ed.), *Founding Fathers of Social Science*, London, 1969.

[12] *See* their journal *Le Producteur*, Vols. I–IV, *passim*.

preclassical society and the Christian Middle Ages). The modern critical period, originating with the Reformation, was, the Saint-Simonians believed, the penultimate stage of human progress, heralding a future organic era of 'universal association' in which 'the organization of the future will be final because only then will society be formed directly for progress'. They used *individualisme* to refer to the pernicious and 'negative' ideas underlying the evils of the modern critical epoch, whose 'disorder, atheism, individualism, and egoism' they contrasted with the prospect of 'order, religion, association and devotion'. The 'philosophers of the eighteenth century'—men such as Helvétius, with his doctrine of 'enlightened self-interest', Locke, Reid, Condillac, Kant, and the 'atheist d'Holbach, the deist Voltaire and Rousseau'—all these 'defenders of individualism' refused to 'go back to a source higher than individual conscience'. They 'considered the individual as the centre' and 'preached egoism', providing an ideological justification for the prevailing anarchy, especially in the economic and political spheres. The 'doctrine of individualism' with its two 'sad deities . . . two creatures of reason—conscience and public opinion' led to 'one political result: opposition to any attempt at organization from a centre of direction for the moral interests of mankind, to hatred of power'.[13]

Partly perhaps because of the extraordinarily pervasive influence of Saint-Simonian ideas, *individualisme* came to be very widely used in the nineteenth century. In France, it usually carried, and indeed still carries, a pejorative connotation, a strong suggestion that to concentrate on the individual is to harm the superior interests of society. The latest edition of the Dictionary of the *Académie Française*[14] defines it simply as 'subordination of the general interest to the individual's

[13] *The Doctrine of Saint-Simon: An Exposition, First Year 1828–9* (1830), tr. G. Iggers, Boston, 1958, pp. 28, 70, 247, 178–80, 182.

[14] Paris, 1932–5.

B

interest', and one recent writer, noting its naturally pejorative sense, has remarked on its 'tinge of "*ubris*", of "*démesure*" ' which 'does not exist in English',[15] while another observes that in France 'until the present day the term individualism has retained much of its former, unfavourable connotations'.[16] It is true that there was a group of French revolutionary republican *Carbonari* in the 1820's who proudly called themselves the 'Société d'Individualistes', and that various individual thinkers adopted the label, among them Proudhon—though even Proudhon saw society as 'a *sui generis* being' and argued that 'outside the group there are only abstractions and phantoms'.[17] From the mid-nineteenth century, liberal Protestants and eventually a few *laissez-faire* liberals started to call themselves individualists and one wrote a comprehensive history of 'economic and social individualism', incorporating a variety of French thinkers[18]— yet the tone was always one of defensive paradox. Few have welcomed the epithet, and many, from Balzac onwards,[19] stressed the opposition between *individualism*, implying anarchy and social atomization, and *individualité*, implying personal independence and self-realization. For the Swiss theologian Alexandre Vinet, these were 'two sworn enemies; the first an obstacle and negation of any society; the latter a principle to which society owes all its savor, life and reality'. The 'progress of individualism' meant 'the relaxation of social

---

[15] L. Moulin, 'On the Evolution of the Meaning of the Word "Individualism" ', *International Social Science Bulletin*, VII (1955), p. 185.

[16] K. W. Swart, ' "Individualism" in the Mid-Nineteenth Century (1826–1860)' , *Journal of the History of Ideas*, XXIII (1962), p. 84.

[17] P.-J. Proudhon, *Lettres sur la philosophie du progrès* (1853), Lettre I, Pts. V and IV in *Oeuvres complètes*, new ed., Paris, 1868–76, Vol. XX, pp. 39–40, 36.

[18] A. Schatz, *L'Individualisme économique et sociale*, Paris, 1907. Cf. H.-L. Follin, 'Quelle est la véritable définition de l'individualisme', *Journal des économistes* (April 15, 1899).

[19] *See* Swart, *art. cit.*, p. 84.

unity because of the increasingly pronounced predominance of egoism', while the 'gradual extinction of individuality' meant 'the increasingly strong inclination for minds . . . to surrender themselves to what is known as public opinion or the spirit of the age'.[20] In general, *individualisme* in French thought points to the sources of social dissolution, though there have been wide divergences concerning the nature of those sources and of the social order they are held to threaten, as well as in the historical frameworks within which they are conceptualized.

For some, individualism resides in dangerous ideas, for others it is social or economic anarchy, a lack of the requisite institutions and norms, for yet others it is the prevalence of self-interested attitudes among individuals. For men of the right, from de Maistre to Charles Maurras, it is all that undermines a traditional, hierarchical social order. Thus Louis Veuillot, the militant Catholic propagandist, wrote in 1843 that 'France has need of religion' which would bring 'harmony, union, patriotis m, confidence, morality. . .':

The evil which plagues France is not unknown; everyone agrees in giving it the same name: *individualism*.

It is not difficult to see that a country where individualism reigns is no longer in the normal conditions of society, since society is the union of minds and interests, and individualism is division carried to the infinite degree.

All for each, each for all, that is society; each for himself, and thus each against all, that is individualism.[21]

Similarly, during the Dreyfus Affair, Ferdinand Brunetière, the strongly *anti-Dreyfusard* literary historian, defended the

[20] Quoted in *ibid.*, pp. 84–5. Cf. Arieli, *Individualism and Nationalism in American Ideology*, Cambridge, Mass., 1964, Ch. X.

[21] L. Veuillot, 'Lettre à M. Villemain' (August 1843) in *Mélanges religieux, historiques, politiques et litéraires* (1842–56), Paris, 1856–60, Ière série, Vol. I, pp. 132–3.

army and the social order, which he saw as threatened by 'individualism' and 'anarchy', and poured scorn on those intellectuals who had presumed to doubt the justice of Dreyfus's trial. Individualism, he wrote, was

the great sickness of the present time. . . . Each of us has confidence only in himself, sets himself up as the sovereign judge of every-thing . . . when intellectualism and individualism reach this degree of self-infatuation, one must expect them to be or become nothing other than *anarchy*. . . .[22]

Among socialists, individualism has typically been contrasted with an ideal, co-operative social order, variously described as 'association', 'harmony', 'socialism' and 'communism'; the term here refers to the economic doctrine of *laissez-faire* and to the anarchy, social atomization and exploitation produced by industrial capitalism. Pierre Leroux, aiming at a new humanitarian and libertarian socialism, used it to mean the principle, proclaimed by political economy, of 'everyone for himself, and . . . all for riches, nothing for the poor', which atomized society and made men into 'rapacious wolves';[23] 'society', he maintained, 'is entering a new era in which the general tendency of the laws will no longer have individualism as its end, but association'.[24] For Constantin Pecqueur, 'the remedy lies in association precisely because the abuse springs from individualism'[25] and the utopian Etienne Cabet wrote that

[22] F. Brunetière, 'Après le procès', *Revue des deux mondes*, LXVII (15 March 1898), p. 445. *See* the author's article: 'Durkheim's "Individualism and the Intellectuals," ', *Political Studies*, XVII (1969), pp. 14–19.

[23] (1832 and 1833) Quoted in Arieli, *op. cit.*, p. 233.

[24] (1841) Quoted in J. Dubois, *Le Vocabulaire politique et sociale en France de 1869 à 1872*, Paris, 1962, p. 220.

[25] (1840) Quoted in *ibid.*, p. 322.

Two great systems have divided and polarized Humanity ever since the beginning of the world: that of Individualism (or egoism, or personal interest), and that of Communism (or association, or the general interest, or the public interest).[26]

Similarly the conspiratorial revolutionary Auguste Blanqui asserted that 'Communism is the protector of the individual, individualism his extermination'.[27]

Other socialists used the term in more complex ways. Louis Blanc saw individualism as a major cultural principle, encompassing Protestantism, the Bourgeoisie and the Enlightenment, bringing a historically necessary, though false and incomplete, freedom. Its progressive aspect was a new self-assertion, a new independence of traditional structures and rejection of Authority in the religious, economic and intellectual spheres; but it needed to be transcended and completed, pointing towards a future age of socialist Fraternity. In Blanc's own words:

Three great principles divide the world and history: Authority, Individualism and Fraternity.

The principle of individualism is that which, taking man out of society, makes him sole judge of what surrounds him and of himself, gives him a heightened sense of his rights without showing him his duties, abandons him to his own powers, and, for the whole of government, proclaims *laisser-faire*.

Individualism, inaugurated by Luther, has developed with an irresistible force, and, dissociated from the religious factor . . . it governs the present; it is the spiritual principle of things.

. . . individualism is important in having achieved a vast progress. To provide breathing-space and scope to human thought repressed for so long, to intoxicate it with pride and audacity; to submit to the judgement of every mind the totality of traditions, centuries, their achievements, their beliefs; to place man in an isolation full of anxieties, full of perils, but sometimes also full of majesty, and to

---

[26] (1845) Quoted in *ibid.*   [27] (1869) Quoted in *ibid.*, p. 267.

enable him to resolve personally, in the midst of an immense struggle, in the uproar of a universal debate, the problem of his happiness and his destiny . . . this is by no means an achievement without grandeur, and it is the achievement of individualism. One must therefore speak of it with respect and as a necessary transition.[28]

Again, the disciples of Charles Fourier denied any basic opposition between individualism and socialism,[29] while at the end of the century, Jean Jaurès argued that 'socialism is the logical completion of individualism',[30] a formula echoed by Émile Durkheim, who saw a kind of centralized guild socialism as a means of 'completing, extending and organizing individualism'.[31] For all these socialist thinkers, individualism signified the autonomy, freedom and sacredness of the individual— values which had hitherto taken a negative, oppressive and anarchic form but could henceforth only be preserved within a co-operative and rationally-organized social order.

French liberals also spoke of individualism, but they charac- teristically saw it as a threat to a pluralist social order, with minimum state intervention and maximum political liberty. Benjamin Constant, perhaps the most eloquent exponent of classical liberalism, was clearly groping for the word when he observed that 'when all are isolated by egoism, there is nothing but dust, and at the advent of a storm, nothing but mire'.[32]

[28] From his *Histoire de la Révolution française* (1846), quoted in R. Koebner, 'Zur Begriffbildung der Kulturgeschichte: II: Zur Geschichte des Begriffs "Individualismus" (Jacob Burckhardt, Wilhelm von Humboldt und die französiche Soziologie)', *Historische Zeitschrift*, CXLIX (1934), p. 269.

[29] *See* Swart, *art. cit.*, p. 85.

[30] J. Jaurès, 'Socialisme et liberté', *Revue de Paris*, XXIII (Dec. 1898), p. 499.

[31] É. Durkheim, 'Individualism and the Intellectuals' (1898), tr. S. and J. Lukes, *Political Studies*, XVII (1969), p. 29. Cf. Lukes, 'Durkheim's "Individualism and the Intellectuals" ', *op. cit.*

[32] Quoted in H. Marion, 'Individualisme', *La Grande Encyclopédie*, Paris, n.d., Vol. XX.

It was, however, that aristocratic observer of early nineteenth-century America, Alexis de Tocqueville, who developed its most distinctive and influential liberal meaning in France. For Tocqueville, individualism was the natural product of demo-cracy ('Individualism is of democratic origin and threatens to develop in so far as conditions are equalized'), involving the apathetic withdrawal of individuals from public life into a private sphere and their isolation from one another, with a consequent weakening of social bonds. Such a development, Tocqueville thought, offered dangerous scope for the un-checked growth of the political power of the state.

More specifically, 'individualism'—a 'recent expression to which a new idea has given birth'—was 'a deliberate and peaceful sentiment which disposes each citizen to isolate himself from the mass of his fellows and to draw apart with his family and friends', abandoning 'the wider society to itself'. At first, it 'saps only the virtues of public life; but, in the long run, it attacks and destroys all others and is eventually absorbed into pure egoism'. In contrast to aristocratic society, in which men were 'linked closely to something beyond them and are often disposed to forget themselves' and which 'formed of all the citizens a long chain reaching from the peasant to the king', democracy 'breaks the chain and sets each link apart', and 'the bond of human affections extends and relaxes'. With increasing social mobility, the continuity of the generations is destroyed; as classes become fused, 'their members become indifferent and as if strangers to one another'; and as individuals become increasingly self-sufficient, 'they become accustomed to considering themselves always in isolation, they freely imagine that their destiny is entirely in their own hands'. Democracy, Tocqueville concluded,

not only makes each man forget his forefathers, but it conceals from him his descendants and separates him from his contemporaries; it ceaselessly throws him back on himself alone and threatens finally to confine him entirely in the solitude of his own heart.[33]

Individualism for Tocqueville thus sprang from the lack of intermediary groups to provide a framework for the individual and protection against the State. (As for the Americans, they only avoided its destructive consequences because of their free institutions and active citizenship: they conquered individualism with liberty.) It was, moreover, a peculiarly modern evil: 'Our fathers', Tocqueville wrote,

did not have the word 'individualism', which we have coined for our own use, because in their time there was indeed no individual who did not belong to a group and who could be considered as absolutely alone.[34]

No less diverse than these conceptions of the sources and the dangers of individualism have been the historical frameworks within which French thinkers have placed it. It is variously traced to the Reformation, the Renaissance, the Enlightenment, the Revolution, to the decline of the aristocracy or the Church or traditional religion, to the Industrial Revolution, to the growth of capitalism or democracy, but, as we have seen, there is wide agreement in seeing it as an evil and a threat to social cohesion. Perhaps the role of 'individualisme' in French thought is partly due to the very success of 'individualist' legislation at the time of the Revolution,[35] the elimination of intermediary

[33] A. de Tocqueville, *De la Démocratie en Amérique* (1835), Bk. II, Pt. II, Ch. II in *Oeuvres complètes*, ed. J. P. Mayer, Paris, 1951–, tome I, II, pp. 104–106.

[34] *L'Ancien Régime et la Révolution* (1856), Bk. II, Ch. IX in *ibid.*, tome II, 1, p. 158.

[35] *See* R. R. Palmer, 'Man and Citizen: Applications of Individualism in the French Revolution' in *Essays in Political Theory presented to G. H. Sabine*, Ithaca, 1948.

groups and bodies in the society, and the ensuing political and administrative centralization of the country. The basis for this had been laid, as Tocqueville observed, in the municipal and fiscal policies of the French kings in the seventeenth and eighteenth centuries, which had systematically prevented the growth of spontaneous, organised activities and informal groupings.[36] One can even reasonably postulate that the lack of such activities and groupings is a basic and distinctive French cultural trait.[37]

However that may be, the mainstream of French thought, above all in the nineteenth century, has expressed by '*individualisme*' what Durkheim identified by the twin concepts of 'anomie 'and 'egoism'[38]—the social, moral and political isolation of individuals, their dissociation from social purposes and social regulation, the breakdown of social solidarity. General de Gaulle was using it in its paradigmatic French sense when in his New Year's broadcast to the nation on 31 December 1968, recalling the *Evénements* of May that year, he observed:

At the same time, it is necessary that we surmount the moral malaise which—above all among us by reason of our individualism— is inherent in modern mechanical and materialist civilisation. Otherwise, the fanatics of destruction, the doctrinaires of negation, the specialists in demagogy, will once more have a good opportunity to exploit bitterness in order to provoke agitation, while their sterility, which they have the derisory insolence to call revolution, can lead to nothing else than the dissolution of everything into nothingness, or else to the loss of everything under the grinding oppression of totalitarianism.[39]

[36] See *L'Ancien Régime et la Révolution*, Bk. II, Chs. 3, 6, 9, 12.
[37] See M. Crozier, *The Bureaucratic Phenomenon*, London, 1964, esp. Ch. 8.
[38] See his *Suicide* (1897), tr. J. A. Spaulding and G. Simpson, Glencoe, Ill., 1951.
[39] *Le Monde*, 2 Jan. 1969.

Despite wide divergences in views about the causes of social dissolution and the nature of an acceptable or desirable social order, the underlying perspective conveyed by the term is unmistakable.

French:
negative!
dissolution ↑
threat to
organic
association

CHAPTER 2

Germany

This characteristically French meaning was certainly subject to cultural diffusion beyond the borders of France. It was, for instance, adopted by Friedrich List, precursor of the German Historical School of economics and advocate of economic nationalism, who used it in the sense developed by the Saint-Simonians and the socialists. List's major work, *The National System of Political Economy*,[1] written in Paris, stressed the organic nature of society and the economy, and the historical and national framework of economic activity; and it attacked the classical economists for abstracting economic life from its social context. Thus List accused classical economics, which supported free trade and *laissez-faire*, of *Kosmopolitismus*, *Materialismus*, *Partikularismus* and, above all, of *Individualismus*—sacrificing the welfare of the national community to the individual acquisition of wealth.

There is, however, quite distinct from this French use of the term, another use whose characteristic reference is German. This is the Romantic idea of 'individuality' (*Individualität*), the notion of individual uniqueness, originality, self-realization—what the Romantics called *Eigentümlichkeit*—in contrast to the rational, universal and uniform standards of the Enlightenment, which they saw as 'quantitative', 'abstract' and therefore

[1] (1841) tr., London, 1928.

sterile. The Romantics themselves did not use the term '*Indi-vidualismus*', but it came to be used in this sense from the 1840's when a German liberal, Karl Brüggemann, contrasted with its negative French meaning, as found in List, that of a desirable and characteristically German 'infinite' and 'whole-souled' individualism, signifying 'the infinite self-confidence of the individual aiming to be personally free in morals and in truth'.[2]

Thereafter, the term soon became, in this, chiefly German, use, virtually synonymous with the idea of individuality, which had originated in the writings of Wilhelm von Humboldt, Novalis, Friedrich Schlegel and Friedrich Schleiermacher. Thus Georg Simmel wrote of the 'new individualism' which he opposed to 'eighteenth-century individualism' with its 'notion of atomized and basically undifferentiated individuals'; the new, German, individualism was 'the individualism of difference, with the deepening of individuality to the point of the individual's incomparability, to which he is "called" both in his nature and in his achievement'. The individual became 'this specific, irreplaceable, given individual' and was '*called* or destined to realize his own incomparable image'. The 'new individualism', Simmel wrote,

might be called qualitative, in contrast with the quantitative indi-vidualism of the eighteenth century. Or it might be labeled the individualism of uniqueness (*Einzigkeit*) as against that of singleness (*Einzelheit*). At any rate, Romanticism was perhaps the broadest channel through which it reached the consciousness of the nineteenth century. Goethe had created its artistic, and Schleiermacher its metaphysical basis: Romanticism supplied its sentimental experiential foundation.[3]

[2] K. H. Brüggemann, *Dr. Lists nationales System der politischen Ökonomie*, Berlin, 1842, quoted in Koebner, *art. cit.*, p. 282.

[3] G. Simmel, 'Individual and Society in Eighteenth- and Nineteenth-Century Views of Life: an Example of Philosophical Sociology' (1917), tr. in *The Sociology of George Simmel*, tr. and ed. K. H. Wolff, Glencoe, Ill.,

The German idea of individuality has had a remarkable history. Having begun as a cult of individual genius and originality, especially as applied to the artist, stressing the conflict between individual and society and the supreme value of subjectivity, solitude and introspection, it developed along various lines. In one direction, it led to an uninhibited quest for eccentricity and to the purest egoism and social nihilism. This development found perhaps its most extreme expression in the thought of Max Stirner, whose 'individualism' amounted to an amoral and anti-intellectualistic vision of freely co-operating and self-assertive egoists. For Stirner,

I, the egoist, have not at heart the welfare of this 'human society'. I sacrifice nothing to it. I only utilize it: but to be able to utilize it completely I must transform it rather into my property amd my creature—i.e., I must annihilate it and form in its place the Union of Egoists.[4]

The main development, however, of the idea of individuality was in the direction of a characteristically German *Weltanschauung*, or cosmology, a total view of the (natural and social) world, fundamentally in conflict with the essentially humanist and rationalist thought typical of the rest of Western civilization. In a justly famous essay, Ernst Troeltsch contrasted the two systems of thought, the 'west-European' and the German: the former 'an eternal, rational and divinely ordained system of Order, embracing both morality and law'; the latter 'individual, living and perpetually new incarnations of an historically creative Mind'. Thus,

---

1950, pp. 78–83. Cf. L. Furst, *Romanticism in Perspective*, London, 1969, Pt. I: 'Individualism'.

[4] M. Stirner, *The Ego and its Own: The Case of the Individual against Authority* (1844), tr. S. T. Byington, London and New York, 1907, quoted in G. Woodcock, *Anarchism*, London, 1963, p. 93. Cf. V. Basch, *L'Individualisme Anarchiste: Max Stirner*, Paris, 1904.

Those who believe in an eternal and divine Law of Nature, the Equality of man, and a sense of Unity pervading mankind, and who find the essence of Humanity in these things, cannot but regard the German doctrine as a curious mixture of mysticism and brutality. Those who take an opposite view—who see in history an ever-moving stream, which throws up unique individualities as it moves, and is always shaping individual structures on the basis of a law which is always new—are bound to consider the west-European world of ideas as a world of cold rationalism and equalitarian atomism, a world of superficiality and Pharisaism.[5]

Friedrich Meinecke summed up the revolution in thought which he saw Romanticism as bringing to Western civilization in the following way:

Out of this deepening individualism of uniqueness, there henceforth arose everywhere in Germany, in various different forms, a new and more living image of the State, and also a new picture of the world. The whole world now appeared to be filled with individuality, each individuality, whether personal or supra-personal, governed by its own characteristic principle of life, and both nature and History constituting what Friedrich Schlegel called an 'abyss of individuality' . . . Individuality everywhere, the identity of mind and nature, and through this identity an invisible but strong bond unifying the otherwise boundless diversity and abundance of individual phenomena—these were the new and powerful ideas which now burst forth in Germany in so many different ways.[6]

In particular, the personal 'individualism' of the early Romantics very soon became transformed into an organic and nationalistic theory of community, each unique and self-

[5] E. Troeltsch, 'The Ideas of Natural Law and Humanity in World Politics' (1922) in O. Gierke, *Natural Law and the Theory of Society, 1500–1800,* tr. E. Barker, Boston, 1957, p. 204.

[6] F. Meinecke, *Die Idee der Staatsräson* (1924) in *Werke,* Munich, 1957–62, Vol. I, p. 425.

sufficient, according to which, as one recent scholar has said, the individual was 'fated to merge with and become rooted in nature and the Volk' and would thus be 'able to find his self-expression and his individuality'.[7] Moreover, individuality was ascribed no longer merely to persons, but to supra-personal forces, especially the nation or the state. Meinecke paints a vivid picture of this transformation:

This new sense for what was individual resembled a fire which was capable of consuming, not all at once, but gradually, every sphere of life. At first, it seized only the flimsiest and most inflammable materials—the subjective life of the individual, the world of art and poetry; but then it went on to consume heavier substances, above all the state.[8]

The same progression from the individuality of the person to that of the nation or state occurred in countless German thinkers of the early nineteenth century—notably, in Fichte, Schelling, Schleiermacher and even Hegel. The state and society were no longer regarded as rational constructions, the result of contractual arrangements between individuals in the manner of the Enlightenment; they were 'super-personal creative forces, which build from time to time out of the material of particular individuals, a spiritual Whole, and on the basis of that Whole proceed from time to time to create the particular political and social institutions which embody and incarnate its significance'.[9] As Simmel wrote, the 'total organism' of society 'shifts, so to speak into a location high above [individuals]' and, accordingly, 'this individualism, which restricts freedom to a purely inward sense of the term, easily acquires an anti-liberal tendency'; it is 'the complete antithesis of

[7] G. L. Mosse, *The Crisis of German Ideology*, London, 1966, p. 15. Compare Mannheim's attempt to explain the conservative direction taken by Romanticism in Mannheim, 'Conservative Thought', *loc. cit.*

[8] *Op. cit.*, p. 426.   [9] Troeltsch, *loc. cit.*, pp. 210–11.

eighteenth-century individualism which . . . could not even conceive the idea of a collective as an organism that unifies heterogeneous elements.[10]

While the characteristically French sense of 'individualism' is negative, signifying individual isolation and social dissolution, the characteristically German sense is thus positive, signifying individual self-fulfilment and (except among the earliest Romantics) the organic unity of individual and society. The distinction was drawn with particular force by Thomas Mann, in a passage written at the close of the First World War, which argues that German life reconciles the individual and society, freedom and obligation:

It remains the uniqueness of German individualism that it is entirely compatible with ethical socialism, which is called 'state socialism' but which is quite distinct from the philosophy of the rights of man and Marxism. For it is only the individualism of the Enlightenment, the liberal individualism of the West, which is incompatible with the social principle.

The German variety, Mann thought, 'includes the freedom of the individual'. To 'reject the individualistic Enlightenment does not amount to a demand for the submergence of the individual in society and the state': the German theory of organic community protected freedom, whereas ideas deriving from the Enlightenment (among which Mann included Marxism) led to Jacobinism, state absolutism, political tyranny. 'Organism' was a word that is 'true to life', for 'an organism is more than the sum of its parts, and that more is its spirit, its life'.[11] Here one can see that individualism is not thought as by the French, to endanger social solidarity, but to be its supreme realization.

[10] *Op. cit.*, p. 82.
[11] T. Mann, *Betrachtungen eines Unpolitischen*, Berlin, 1918, p. 267.

CHAPTER 3

Jacob Burckhardt

A striking and influential synthesis of French and German meanings of 'individualism' is to be found (appropriately enough) in the work of the Swiss historian, Jacob Burckhardt. A central theme of Burckhardt's *The Civilization of the Renaissance in Italy*[1] was the growth of 'individualism'. Summing up the 'principal features in the Italian character of that time', Burckhardt maintained that its 'fundamental vice . . . was at the same time a condition of its greatness, namely, excessive individualism.'[2] The second part of the work is entitled 'The Development of the Individual' and, in general, Burckhardt treated the Italians of the Renaissance as a people 'who have emerged from the half-conscious life of the race and become themselves individuals'.[3]

Schematically, one can say that Burckhardt's use of 'individualism' combines the notion of the aggressive self-assertion of individuals freed from an externally-given framework of authority (as found in Louis Blanc) and that of the individual's withdrawal from society into a private existence (as in Tocqueville) with the early Romantic idea, most clearly expressed by Humboldt, of the full and harmonious developments of the individual personality, seen as representing humanity and

[1] (1860) tr. S. G. C. Middlemore, London, 1955. *See* Koebner, *art. cit.*
[2] *Ibid.*, p. 279.
[3] *Ibid.*, p. 200.

C

pointing towards its highest cultural development. The Italian of the Renaissance was for Burckhardt 'the firstborn among the sons of modern Europe'[4] in virtue of the autonomy of his morality, his cultivation of privacy and the individuality of his character.

'The individual', Burckhardt wrote,

first inwardly casts off the authority of a State which, as a fact, is in most cases tyrannical and illegitimate, and what he thinks and does is now, rightly or wrongly, called treason. The sight of victorious egotism in others drives him to defend his own right by his own arm. . . . In face of all objective facts, of laws and restraints of whatever kind, he retains the feeling of his own sovereignty, and in each single instance forms his decision independently, according as honour or interest, passion or calculation, revenge or renunciation, gain the upper hand in his own mind.[5]

As to privacy, Burckhardt wrote of 'the different tendencies and manifestations of private life . . . thriving in the fullest vigour and variety' and cited 'Agnolo Pandolfini (d. 1446), whose work on domestic economy is the first complete programme of a developed private life'. 'The private man', he argued, 'indifferent to politics, and busied partly with serious pursuits, partly with the interests of a *dilettante*, seems to have been first fully formed in these despotisms of the fourteenth century'.[6] Finally, he identified the 'impulse to the highest individual development' and saw Italy at the close of the thirteenth century as beginning to 'swarm with individuality; the ban upon human personality was dissolved; and a thousand figures meet us each in his own special shape and dress'. Dante, 'through the wealth of individuality which he set forth', was 'the most national herald of his time'; much of Burckhardt's book treats

[4] *Ibid.*, p. 80.   [5] *Ibid.*, p. 279.
[6] *Ibid.*, pp. 82–3.

of 'this unfolding of the treasures of human nature in literature and art'. An acute and practised eye could trace

the increase in the number of complete men during the fifteenth century. Whether they had before them as a conscious object the harmonious development of their spiritual and material existence is hard to say, but several of them attained it, so far as is consistent with the imperfection of all that is earthly.[7]

It is worth adding that for Burckhardt this growth of individualism was, as for so many philosophers of history, no accident, but a 'historical necessity'. Transmitted by Italian culture, and infusing the other nations of Europe, it

has constituted since then the higher atmosphere which they breathe. In itself it is neither good nor bad, but necessary; within it has grown up a modern standard of good and evil—a sense of moral responsibility—which is essentially different from that which was familiar to the Middle Ages.[8]

[7] *Ibid.*, pp. 81–4.

[8] *Ibid.*, p. 279. Earlier in his life Burckhardt wrote (in a letter to Schauenburg, 28 Feb. 1846) that 'states are not built with men like me . . . I mean to be a good private individual'. But in his later life he became disillusioned with 'individualism', remarking: 'You know, as far as individualism is concerned, I hardly believe in it any more, but I don't say so, it gives them so much pleasure' (cited by W. Kaegi in introduction to *Ernst Walser: Gesammelte Studien zur Geistesgeschichte der Renaissance*, 1932, p. xxxvii). For discussion, *see* Kaegi's *Burckhardt*, Basel/Stuttgart, 1956, Vol. III, pp. 712f. For the information in this note I am indebted to Peter Burke.

CHAPTER 4

America

It was in the United States that 'individualism' primarily came to celebrate capitalism and liberal democracy. It became a symbolic catchword of immense ideological significance, expressing all that has at various times been implied in the philosophy of natural rights, the belief in free enterprise, and the American Dream. It expressed, in fact, the operative ideals of nineteenth- and early twentieth-century America (and indeed continues to play a major ideological role), advancing a set of universal claims seen as incompatible with the parallel claims of the socialism and communism of the Old World. It referred, not to the sources of social dissolution or the painful transition to a future harmonious social order, nor to the cultivation of uniqueness or the organic community, but rather to the actual or imminent realization of the final stage of human progress in a spontaneously cohesive society of equal individual rights, limited government, *laissez-faire*, natural justice and equal opportunity, and individual freedom, moral development and dignity. Naturally it carried widely varying connotations in differing contexts and at different times.

It was imported, in the negative French sense, *via* the writings of various Europeans, among them the socialists, as well as Tocqueville, List and the Saint-Simonian Michel Chevalier, whose *Lettres sur l'Amérique du Nord* (1836) contrasted the anarchic individualism of the Yankees with the more socially-inclined and organizable French. Already in 1839, an article in the *United States Magazine and Democratic Review* identified it positively with national values and ideals seen in evolutionary and universal terms. 'The course of civilization', it argued,

is the progress of man from a state of savage individualism to that of an individualism more elevated, moral and refined. . . . The last order of civilization, which is democratic, received its first permanent existence in this country. . . . The peculiar duty of this country has been to exemplify and embody a civilization in which the rights, freedom, and mental and moral growth of individual men should be made the highest end of all social restrictions and laws.[1]

This abrupt change in the evaluative significance of the term is strikingly illustrated in one of the earliest American discussions of Tocqueville's *Democracy in America*, by a Transcendentalist writer in the *Boston Quarterly Review*. The writer, inaccurately but significantly, expounded Tocqueville's concept of individualism as expressing 'that strong confidence in self, or reliance upon one's own exertion and resources' and as 'the strife of all our citizens for wealth and distinction of *their own*, and their contempt of reflected honours'. 'Individualism', he continued,

has its immutable laws . . . which . . . when allowed to operate without let or hindrance . . . must in the end assimilate the species, and evolve all the glorious phenomena of original and eternal *order*; —that order which exists in man himself, and alone vivifies and sustains him.[2]

[1] 'The Course of Civilization', *United States Magazine and Democratic Review*, VI (1839), pp. 208 ff, 211, quoted in Arieli, *op. cit.*, pp. 191–2.
[2] 'Catholicism', *Boston Quarterly Review*, IV (1841), pp. 320 ff, quoted in Arieli, *op. cit.*, p. 199.

'Individualism' had, by the end of the Civil War, acquired an important place in the vocabulary of American ideology. Indeed, even those who criticized American society, from New England Transcendentalists to the Single Taxers and the Populists, often did so in the name of individualism. The term acquired differing layers of meaning under the successive influences of New England Puritanism, the Jeffersonian tradition and natural rights philosophy; Unitarianism, Transcendentalism and evangelicalism; the need of the North to develop an ideological defence against the challenge of the South; the immensely popular evolutionary and *laissez-faire* ideas of Herbert Spencer and the growth of Social Darwinism; and the permanent and continuing impetus of alternative, European-born ideologies. The course of this development has been admirably traced in Yehoshua Arieli's book, *Individualism and Nationalism in American Ideology*,[3] which rightly treats the American version of 'individualism' as a symbol of national identification. As Arieli concludes,

Individualism supplied the nation with a rationalization of its characteristic attitudes, behaviour patterns and aspirations. It endowed the past, the present and the future with the perspective of unity and progress. It explained the peculiar social and political organization of the nation—unity in spite of heterogeneity—and it pointed towards an ideal of social organization in harmony with American experience. Above all, individualism expressed the universalism and idealism most characteristic of the national consciousness. This concept evolved in contradistinction to socialism, the universal and messianic character of which it shared.[4]

It can, indeed, be argued that the lack of a socialist tradition in America is in part a consequence of the very pervasiveness of individualism.

---

[3] *See* note 20, p. 9.   [4] *Op. cit.*, pp. 345–6.

A perusal of the various American uses of the term reveals a quite distinctive range of connotations. For Emerson, contemplating the failure of Brook Farm, individualism, which he endowed with an exalted moral and religious significance, had 'never been tried';[5] it was the route to perfection—a spontaneous social order of self-determined, self-reliant and fully-developed individuals. 'The union', he wrote, 'is only perfect when all the uniters are isolated. . . . Each man, if he attempts to join himself to others, is on all sides cramped and diminished. . . . The Union must be ideal in actual individualism.'[6] Society was tending towards a morally superior voluntary social order, a 'free and just commonwealth' in which 'property rushes from the idle and imbecile to the industrious, brave and persevering;[7] For the historian John William Draper, writing immediately after the Civil War, in celebration of the social system of the North, its

population was in a state of unceasing activity; there was a corporeal and mental restlessness. Magnificent cities in all directions were arising; the country was intersected with canals, railroads . . . companies for banking, manufacturing, commercial purposes, were often concentrating many millions of capital. There were all kinds of associations . . . churches, hospitals, schools abounded. The foreign commerce at length rivaled that of the most powerful nations of Europe. This wondeful spectacle of social development was the result of INDIVIDUALISM; operating in an unbounded theatre of action. Everyone was seeking to do all that he could for himself.[8]

[5] R. W. Emerson, *Journals* (1846), Cambridge, Mass., 1909–14, Vol. VII, pp. 322–3.

[6] R. W. Emerson, 'New England Reformers' (1844) in *Complete Writings*, New York, 1929, Vol. I, pp. 317–18.

[7] 'Wealth' (1860) in *ibid.*, p. 551.

[8] J. W. Draper, *History of the American Civil War*, 3 Vols., New York, 1868–70, Vol. I, pp. 207–8.

And for Walt Whitman, likewise celebrating the democratic
system of the North, it incarnated the progressive force of
modern history—'the singleness of man, individualism',[9]
reconciling liberty and social justice.

In the hands of the Social Darwinists, such as William
Graham Sumner, 'individualism' acquired a harsher and
altogether less idealistic significance. Sumner, who maintained
that 'liberty, inequality, survival of the fittest . . . carries society
forward and favours all its best members',[10] offered a purport-
edly scientific rationale for a ruthlessly competitive society where
the individual 'has all his chances left open that he makes out
of himself all there is in him. This is individualism and atomism'.[11] In this context, the influence of Herbert Spencer's
doctrines as a justification for ruthless rivalry in business and
unscrupulous dealings in politics was immense; he was widely
seen as 'the shining light of evolution and individualism'.[12]
These ideas entered into an evolving ideology of private
enterprise and *laissez-faire*, postulating absolute equality of
opportunity and the claim that private accumulation leads to
public welfare. The word was used in this sense by Andrew
Carnegie, and by Henry Clews, author of *The Wall Street
Point of View* (1900), who spoke of 'that system of Individualism
which guards, protects and encourages competition', whose
spirit was 'the American Spirit—the love of freedom,—of free
industry,—free and unfettered opportunity. . . .'[13] It was also
used favourably by Theodore Roosevelt, Woodrow Wilson

---

[9] W. Whitman, *Democratic Vistas* (1871) in *Complete Prose Works*,
Philadelphia, 1891, Vol. II, p. 67.

[10] Quoted in R. Hofstadter, *Social Darwinism in American Thought*, revised
cloth ed., New York, 1959, p. 51, *q.v. passim.*, esp. ch. 3.

[11] W. G. Summer, *Earth Hunger and Other Essays*, New Haven, 1913, pp.
127–8.

[12] J. R. Commons, quoted in Hofstadter, *op. cit.*, p. 34.

[13] H. Clews, *Individualism versus Socialism*, New York, 1907, pp. 1–3.

and William Jennings Bryan. Despite countertrends to the
'Gospel of Wealth' and the 'Gospel of Success', the term
continued to have wide currency until a temporary eclipse
during the Depression and the New Deal. It was in 1928 that
Herbert Hoover gave his famous campaign speech on the
'American system of rugged individualism'; yet the term
regained its resonance, as can be seen by the sales of the writings
of the contemporary novelist-'philosopher', Ayn Rand, in
defence of 'reason, individualism and capitalism'.

In short, with regard to the American sense of 'individualism'
James Bryce was accurate when he observed that, throughout
their history,

individualism, the love of enterprise, and pride in personal freedom,
have been deemed by Americans not only their choicest, but their
petition; they have accepted the economic virtues of capitalist culture as

14 J. Bryce, *The American Commonwealth*, London and New York, 1888,
Vol. II, p. 404. Cf. Richard Hofstadter: 'However much at odds on specific
issues, the major political traditions have shared a belief in the rights of
property, the philosophy of economic individualism, the value of competition; they have accepted the economic virtues of capitalist culture as
necessary qualities of man' (*The American Political Tradition* (Vintage Books),
New York, 1954, p. viii).

CHAPTER 5

England

In England, the term has played a smaller role, as an epithet for nonconformity in religion, for the sterling qualities of self-reliant Englishmen, especially among the nineteenth-century middle-classes, and for features common to the various strands of English liberalism. French and German influences can, of course, also be found. Its first use was in Henry Reeve's translation of Tocqueville's *De la Démocratie en Amérique* in 1840. The word was also used in the pejorative French sense by a great number of thinkers, but especially socialists, to refer to the evils of capitalist competition. Thus Robert Owen, in specifying his co-operative socialist ideals, argued that to 'effect these changes there must be . . . a new organization of society, on the principle of *attractive* union, instead of *repulsive individualism* . . .',[1] while John Stuart Mill (who was much influenced by the Saint-Simonians) asserted that

the moral objection to competition, as arming one human being against another, making the good of each depend upon evil to others, making all who have anything to gain or lose, live in the midst of enemies, by no means deserves the disdain with which it is treated by some of the adversaries of socialism. . . . Socialism, as long as it attacks the existing individualism, is easily triumphant; its weakness hitherto is in what it proposes to substitute.[2]

[1] R. Owen, *Moral World* (1845), quoted in Arieli, *op. cit.*, p. 406.

[2] J. S. Mill, *Newman's Political Economy* (1851) in *Collected Works*, Toronto and London, 1963–, Vol. V, p. 444.

Mill, expounding, not unsympathetically, the ideas of 'the present Socialists', wrote that, in their eyes,

the very foundation of human life as at present constituted, the very principle on which the production and repartition of all material products is now carried on, is essentially vicious and anti-social. It is the principle of individualism, competition, each one for himself and against all the rest. It is grounded on opposition of interests, not harmony of interests, and under it every one is required to find his place by a struggle, by pushing others back or being pushed back by them. Socialists consider this system of private war (as it may be termed) between every one and every one, especially fatal in an economical point of view and in a moral.[3]

And the socially-conscious Bishop of Durham, Brooke Foss Westcott argued in 1890 that 'individualism regards humanity as made up of disconnected or warring atoms: socialism regards it as an organic whole, a vital unity formed by the combination of contributing members mutually interdependent'.[4]

As to the German sense, this can be seen in the writings of the Unitarian minister William McCall, claimed as a precursor in expounding 'the doctrine of Individuality' (along with Humboldt, the German Romantics, Goethe and Josiah Warren) by John Stuart Mill.[5] McCall, who was influenced by German Romanticism, wrote declamatory books and pamphlets, such as *Elements of Individualism* (1847) and *Outlines of Individualism* (1853), in which he preached the gospel of a new way of life dominated by the 'Principle of Individualism', which he hoped England would be the first country to adopt.

Among indigenous uses, the term's reference to non-conformity is evident in the condemnation by Gladstone, who

[3] J. S. Mill, *Chapters on Socialism* (1879) in *ibid.*, p. 715.

[4] *The Guardian*, 8 Oct. 1890, quoted in O.E.D.

[5] *See* Mill's Autobiography (1873), paperback ed., New York, 1960, p. 179.

for a time advocated a single state religion, of 'our individualism in religion'[6] and in Matthew Arnold's contrast between the Catholics' ecclesiastical conception of the Eucharist and its origin 'as Jesus founded it' where 'it is the consecration of absolute individualism'.[7] The term's reference to the English character can be seen in Samuel Smiles, that ardent moralist on behalf of the Manchester School of political economy (who helped himself materially by the publication of his precepts). 'The spirit of self-help', he wrote, 'as exhibited in the energetic action of individuals, has in all times been a marked feature of the English character'; even 'the humblest person, who sets before his fellows an example of industry, sobriety and upright honesty of purpose in life, has a present as well as a future influence upon the well-being of his country'. It was this 'energetic individualism which produces the most powerful effects upon the life and action of others, and really constitutes the best practical education'.[8]

It was centrally in reference to English liberalism that 'individualism' came to be mainly used in the latter half of the nineteenth century, in contrast with 'socialism', 'communism' and, especially, 'collectivism'. Thus the *Pall Mall Gazette* in 1888 spoke of holding 'the scales between Individualists and Socialists'[9] and the *Times* in 1896 of 'the individualists' holding 'their own against the encroachments of the State'.[10] In a House of Commons debate in 1923 on 'The Failure of the Capitalist System' (the motion being proposed by Snowden), a leading Liberal, Sir Alfred Mond, defended 'private interest in

[6] W. E. Gladstone, *Church Principles Considered in their Results*, London, 1840, p. 98, quoted in O.E.D.

[7] M. Arnold, *Literature and Dogma* (1873), London, 1876, p. 312, quoted in O.E.D.

[8] S. Smiles, *Self Help* (1859), London, 1958, pp. 38, 39.

[9] 10 Sept. 1888 quoted in O.E.D.

[10] 30 Jan. 1896 quoted in O.E.D.

the means of production and distribution' and 'the benefits of individual initiative', declaring that the country was presented with 'a clear issue between Individualism and Socialism'.[11]

In 1890, Sidney Webb had advanced the case against individualism, meaning by it Manchester Liberalism, and drew up the table on pages 36 and 37 below, contrasting the old individualism with the new socialism.

Oscar Wilde, on the other hand, maintained that 'Socialism itself will be of value simply because it will lead to Individualism'. 'Socialism, Communism or whatever one chooses to call it' would, by converting private property into public wealth, ensure the material well-being of all, but 'for the full development of life to its highest mode of perfection, something more is needed. What is needed is Individualism. If the Socialism is Authoritarian; if there are Governments armed with economic power as they are now with political power; if, in a word, we are to have Industrial Tyrannies, then the last state of man will be worse than the first. At present, in consequence of the existence of private property, a great many people are enabled to develop a certain very limited amount of Individualism'. With the abolition of private property, 'we shall have true, beautiful, healthy individualism'.[12]

Though scarcely used by the political economists and the Benthamites, and though, as we have seen, Mill used it in a different and negative sense, 'individualism' came to be attributed to, and embraced by, the whole spectrum of English liberals, from those advocating the most extreme *laissez-faire* to those supporting quite extensive state intervention. Among the former was Herbert Spencer, concerned to assist the general course of social evolution by arresting the imminent 'drift towards a form of society in which private activities of every

[11] Cited in S. H. Beer, *Modern British Politics*, London, 1965, p. 142.
[12] Oscar Wilde, *The Soul of Man Under Socialism* (1891) in *Oscar Wilde's Plays, Prose Writings and Poems* (Everyman's Library), London, pp. 258–63.

INDIVIDUALIST RADICALISM 1840–1874	SOCIALIST RADICALISM 1889
'That the best government is that which governs least.'	'That the best government is that which can safely and successfully administer most.'
Corollary. Wherever you can make a 'soft place' for a contractor do so.	*Corollary.* Wherever the collective organization of the community can dispense with a contractor or other 'entrepreneur', it should do so.
'That the utmost possible scope should be allowed to individual enterprise in industry.'	'That, wherever possible, industries of widespread public service should be organized and controlled for the public benefit.'
Corollary. The best social use to which you can turn a profitable monopoly is to hand it over to some lucky individual to make a fortune out of it.	*Corollary.* Every industry yielding more than a fair remuneration to the actual managers should be 'municipalized' or 'nationalized' or else specially taxed.
'That open competition and complete freedom from legal restrictions furnish the best guarantees of a healthy industrial community.'	'That only by gradually increasing legal restrictions can the worst competitors be prevented from ousting their better rivals.'
Corollary. John Bright's opinion that adulteration is only a form of competition:	*Corollary.* 'The answer of modern statesmanship is that unfettered individual

INDIVIDUALIST RADICALISM 1840–1874	SOCIALIST RADICALISM 1889
the 'individualism' of Mr. Auberon Herbert.	competition is not a principle to which the regulation of industry may be entrusted.' (Mr. John Morley, 'Life of Cobden,' Vol. I, Ch. XIII, 298.)
'That the desired end of "equality of opportunity" can be ultimately reached by allowing to each person the complete ownership of any riches he may become possessed of.'	'That Political Economy indubitably proves "equality of opportunity" to be absolutely impossible of even approximate attainment, so long as complete private ownership exists in land and other economic monopolies.'
Corollary. The policy of the 'Liberty and Property Defence League.'	*Corollary.* The policy of 'Nationalization' or 'Municipalization' of Land and other economic monopolies.
'That the best possible social state will result from each individual pursuing his own interest in the way he thinks best.'	'That social health is something apart from and above the interest of individuals, and must be consciously pursued as an end in itself.'
Corollary. 'Private vices, public benefits.'	*Corollary.* The study of the science of sociology and of the art of politics.[13]

13 S. Webb, *Socialism in England*, London, 1908, pp. 26–7.

kind, guided by individual wills, are to be replaced by public
activities guided by governmental will', that 'lapse of self-
ownership into ownership by the community, which is
partially implied by collectivism and completely by communism'.[14] Even more extreme than Spencer was Auberon
Herbert, author of *The Voluntaryist Creed* (1906) and editor in
the 1890's of *The Free Life*, where he described his creed as
'thorough-going individualism', advocating among other things
voluntary taxation and education, and 'the open market and
free trade in everything'. At the other end of the scale were
liberals, such as T. H. Green and L. T. Hobhouse, who
favoured positive political action for the promotion of a liberal
society. For Green, individualism was 'the free competitive
action of the individual in relation to the production and
distribution of wealth', as opposed to 'the collective action of
society operating through society or the executive'; he believed
individualism in this sense to be 'a fundamental principle of
human nature and an essential factor of the well-being of
society'.[15] Hobhouse put the matter very clearly: 'to maintain
individual freedom and equality we have to extend the sphere
of social control', and thus 'individualism, when it grapples
with the facts, is driven no small distance along Socialist
lines'.[16]

Perhaps the most influential use was that typified by Dicey,
who equated individualism with Benthamism and utilitarian
Liberalism. For Dicey,

[14] H. Spencer, *Principles of Sociology*, London, 1876–96, Vol. III, p. 594.
For Spencer's first account of his ideas as the philosophy of individualism,
see the introduction to the American edition of his *Social Statics*, New York,
1865, p. x.

[15] Quoted in M. Richter, *The Politics of Conscience: T. H. Green and his
Age*, London, 1964, p. 343.

[16] L. T. Hobhouse, *Liberalism* (1911), (Galaxy book), New York, 1964, p.
54.

Utilitarian individualism, which for many years under the name of liberalism, determined the trend of English legislation, was nothing but Benthamism modified by the experience, the prudence, or the timidity of practical politicians.

The 'individualistic reformers', he wrote, 'opposed anything which shook the obligations of contracts, or, what is at bottom the same thing, limited the contractual freedom of individuals' and, in general, they 'tacitly assumed that each man if left to himself would in the long run be sure to act for his own true interest, and that the general welfare was sufficiently secured if each man were left free to pursue his happiness in his own way, either alone or in combination with his fellows'.[17] 'Individualism' has, in this sense, been widely used in England to mean the absence or minimum of state intervention in the economic and other spheres, and has usually been associated, both by its adherents and its opponents, with classical liberalism.

[17] A. V. Dicey, *Law and Public Opinion in England* (1905), London, 1962, pp. 125, 151, 156.

D

CHAPTER 6

History and the Social Sciences

Historians and social scientists have come to use 'individualism' in a variety of contexts, the range of which it may be useful briefly to indicate. A. D. Lindsay finds in Epicureanism 'many of the elements which make up modern individualism', namely,

the view that society is nothing more than an aggregate of individuals; the doctrine that the state, law and justice are at best necessary evils; a scientific attitude of mind which leads to the acceptance of psychological atomism and hedonism; and a high valuation set on the voluntary association and the relation of contract.[1]

Others, such as Troeltsch, associate individualism with Primitive Christianity;[2] others, like Burckhardt, with the Italian Renaissance; others, following Max Weber and R. H. Tawney, with Protestantism, especially Calvinism, and the rise of capitalism,[3] or with the growth of a 'possessive market society'

[1] A. D. Lindsay, 'Individualism', *Encyclopedia of the Social Sciences*, New York, 1930–35, Vol. VII, p. 676.

[2] *See* E. Troeltsch, *The Social Teaching of the Christian Churches* (1912), New York, 1931, 2 Vols; *see* Vol. I, Ch. I.

[3] *See* M. Weber, *The Protestant Ethic and the Spirit of Capitalism* (1904–5), tr. by T. Parsons, London, 1930; and R. H. Tawney, *Religion and the Rise of Capitalism*, London, 1926.

in seventeenth-century England;[4] others, such as Otto Gierke, with modern natural law theory, from the mid-seventeenth to the early nineteenth century;[5] and yet others, like Meinecke, with the rise of Romanticism.[6] Finally, economists of a doctrinaire liberal kind, such as the Austro-liberals Ludwig von Mises and Friedrich A. Hayek, and the American Milton Friedman adhere to individualism, tracing it back through the neo-classical to the classical economists, and ultimately to Bernard de Mandeville.

It has, indeed, been argued by Hayek that there are two traditions of individualism—'true' and 'false' individualism: the former stemming from Locke, Mandeville and Hume to achieve full status in the work of Josiah Tucker, Ferguson, Smith, and Burke, and passing in the nineteenth century through Tocqueville and Acton; and the latter including mainly French and Continental writers, inspired by cartesian rationalism, such as the Encyclopedists, Rousseau and the Physiocrats, leading, especially through Saint-Simon, to socialism and collectivism; while the Benthamites and philosophical radicals, as well as John Stuart Mill, were influenced by both traditions.[7] Durkheim, on the other hand, argues for a quite different contrast between types of individualism. For him there is a profound difference between 'the narrow utilitarianism and the utilitarian egoism of Spencer and the economists . . . that paltry commercialism which reduces society to nothing more than a vast apparatus of production and exchange', and 'another individualism . . . that of Kant and

---

[4] See C. B. Macpherson, *The Political Theory of Possessive Individualism, Hobbes to Locke*, Oxford, 1962.

[5] See O. Gierke, *Natural Law and the Theory of Society, 1500 to 1800* (1913), tr. E. Barker, Boston, 1957.

[6] See F. Meinecke, *Werke*, Munich, 1957–62, 6 Vols., *passim*.

[7] F. A. Hayek, 'Individualism: True and False' (1946) in Hayek, *Individualism and Economic Order*, London, 1949.

Rousseau, that of the *spiritualistes,* that which the Declaration of the Rights of Man sought, more or less successfully, to translate into formulae. . . .'[8] Lindsay, however, is more generous: according to him,

All modern political theory, except the theory of Bolshevism and of Fascism, is . . . individualistic in that it seeks to find room for and encourage the individual moral judgement and is based on toleration and the maintenance of a system of rights. Most of the differences between modern individualism, strictly so-called, and socialism are differences within these common assumptions.[9]

Similarly, as we have seen, Élie Halévy argues for the view that 'in western society, individualism is the true philosophy'[10] linking individual autonomy, equality of respect and the notion of society as the product of individual wills, and upheld by Roman law, Christian morality, and by Rousseau, Kant and Bentham.

In the face of this immense and confusing variety of usage, the only way forward is through conceptual analysis. Only by attempting to distinguish between the component ideas variously expressed and combined by the term 'individualism' is any clarity likely to be achieved.

[8] É. Durkheim, 'Individualism and the Intellectuals', pp. 20–1.
[9] *Art. cit.*, p. 677.
[10] Halévy, *The Growth of Philosophical Radicalism*, p. 504. *See* Foreword above.

PART TWO

The Basic Ideas of Individualism

It is not, perhaps, superfluous to remark also that the doctrines or tendencies that are designated by familiar names ending in -*ism* or -*ity*, though they occasionally may be, usually are not, units of the sort which the historian of ideas seeks to discriminate. They commonly constitute, rather, compounds to which his method of analysis needs to be applied. Idealism, romanticism, rationalism, transcendentalism, pragmatism—all these trouble-breeding and usually thought-obscuring terms, which one sometimes wishes to see expunged from the vocabulary of the philosopher and the historian altogether, are names of complexes, not of simples—and of complexes in two senses. They stand, as a rule, not for one doctrine, but for several distinct and often conflicting doctrines held by different individuals or groups to whose way of thinking these appellations have been applied, either by themselves or in the traditional terminology of historians; and each of these doctrines, in turn, is likely to be resolvable into simpler elements, often very strangely combined and derivative from a variety of dissimilar motives and historic influences.

ARTHUR O. LOVEJOY[1]

The term 'individualism' embraces the utmost heterogeneity of meanings . . . a thorough, historically-oriented conceptual analysis

[1] A. O. Lovejoy, *The Great Chain of Being: A Study of the History an Idea*, Cambridge, Mass., 1936, pp. 5–6.

would at the present time be of the highest value to scholar
ship.

MAX WEBER[2]

The first task facing the historian of ideas, according to Lovejoy, is 'a task of logical analysis—the discrimination *in* the
texts, and the segregating *out* of the texts, of each of what I
shall call the basic or germinal ideas, the identification of each
of them so that it can be recognized wherever it appears, in
differing contexts, under different labels or phrasings, and in
diverse provinces of thought'.[3] Part Two of this book seeks
to offer only the tentative and sketchy outlines of a general
analysis of the basic or germinal ideas of individualism. A
number of distinctions will be drawn which are often over-
looked. Indeed, a number of these ideas have often been held
to be naturally related to one another precisely because such
distinctions have not been drawn. It is only by drawing them
that one will be in a position to examine the logical and conceptual relations between the ideas; and it is to that task that I
will turn in the third and final Part of this book. Here the aim
is to isolate some of the basic ideas of individualism by indicat-
ing broad conceptual outlines, partly by definition (positive
and negative) and partly by historical allusion, but with no
suggestion that the elements isolated are either mutually exclusive or jointly exhaustive.

[2] M. Weber. *The Protestant Ethic and the Spirit of Capitalism*, p. 222
(amended translation: S. L.).

[3] A. O. Lovejoy, 'The Meaning of Romanticism for the Historian of
Ideas', *Journal of the History of Ideas*, II (1941), p. 262.

CHAPTER 7

The Dignity of Man

First, there is the ultimate moral principle of *the supreme and intrinsic value, or dignity, of the individual human being*, an idea which Lindsay describes as 'the great contribution to individualism' of the New Testament and all Christianity.[1] Earlier Judaism had made the nation of Israel, not the individual human being, the concern of God; though a new conception of a direct relation between God and the individual is adumbrated in the prophets. Thus, in Ezekiel (XVIII: 2–4) one reads:

What mean ye, that ye use this proverb concerning the land of Israel, saying: The fathers have eaten sour grapes, and the children's teeth are set on edge? As I live, saith the Lord God, ye shall not have occasion any more to use this proverb in Israel. Behold, all souls are mine; as the soul of the father, so also the soul of the son is mine: the soul that sinneth, it shall die.

The idea of the individual's supreme worth under the sovereign will of God is clearly set forth in the Gospels, as in such sayings as 'In as much as ye have done it unto one of the least of these my brethren, ye have done it unto me' (Matthew XXV: 40). The clear implication is that national and other social categories are of secondary moral importance: with the

[1] Lindsay, 'Individualism', p. 676.

coming of Christ, 'there is neither Greek nor Jew, circumcision nor uncircumcision, Barbarian, Scythian, bond nor free: but Christ is all and in all' (Colossians III: 11). In its Christian form, centred on God and implying the supreme value of the God-given soul, this idea was reaffirmed at the time of the Reformation, with Luther's and Calvin's preoccupation with the individual's salvation and the sectarian principle that all men are equally children of and under God, each with his own unique purpose.

It had been de-emphasized in the Middle Ages, partly as a function of the overriding importance of law, and of the Church as a legal institution, and partly as a consequence of the organological conception of society, itself rooted in Roman ideas. This point is made clear in Walter Ullmann's *The Individual and Society in the Middle Ages*. Ullmann writes of the 'absorption of the individual by the community or by society' (citing, for example, collective punishments) and stresses the organic conception according to which each individual 'had been allotted a special function which he pursued for the common good' and which amounted to

the theory that the individual did not exist for his own sake, but for the sake of the whole society. This organological thesis was to lead in time to the full-fledged integration theory of the corporate body politic, in which the individual is wholly submerged in society for the sake of the well-being of society itself.

Society was 'one whole and was indivisible, and within it the individual was no more than a part'; indeed the

individual was so infinitesimally small a part that his interests could easily be sacrificed at the altar of the public good, at the altar of society itself, because nothing was more dangerous to society than the corrosion and undermining of the very element which held it together, that is, the faith.

From the medieval point of view, killing an individual who
attacked the faith was no violation of his dignity. In general,
what mattered was 'not the individual, . . . but . . . the office
which the individual occupied', not 'the individual, but society,
the corpus of all individuals'. As Ullmann puts it, 'we move
within a-human non-individualistic precincts': in 'the high
Middle Ages, thinking in the public field concerned itself with
the whole, with society'. The universally prevailing conception
was

the collectivist standpoint—all the individual bodies may and will
die, but what cannot die is the idea of law, the idea of right order,
which holds the public and corporate body together and which
therefore possessed sempiternity.[2]

It has often been suggested that the first major breach in this
way of thinking came with the great nominalist logician
William of Ockham, for whom only particular beings, and in
the social sphere only particular human beings, really exist. It
was, however, with the Renaissance that the idea of the individual's supreme worth was openly proclaimed. Indeed, it was
a favourite theme among the humanists: hence Petrarch's
conclusion that 'nothing is admirable but the soul in comparison
to which if it is great nothing is great',[3] and Gianozzo Manetti's
treatise on *The Dignity and Excellence of Man* and Pico della
Mirandola's famous *Oration on the Dignity of Man*. Hence
Marsilio Ficino could assimilate this idea to a medieval view of
the Great Chain of Being by writing of the human soul as 'the

[2] W. Ullmann, *The Individual and Society in the Middle Ages*, London,
1967, pp. 32, 40, 42, 36–7, 44, 48, 49. Cf. É. Durkheim, 'Deux Lois de
l'évolution pénale', *L'Année sociologique*, IV (1901), pp. 65–95, which makes
much of the evidence of collective punishment in pre-modern societies.
[3] Quoted in P. O. Kristeller, 'The Philosophy of Man in the Italian
Renaissance', *Italica*, XXIV (1947), p. 97.

greatest of all miracles in nature . . . the centre of nature, the middle term of all things, the series of the world, the face of all, the bond and juncture of the universe'.[4]

This first unit-idea of individualism has come to pervade modern ethical and social thought in the West, as Tocqueville predicted when he maintained that the norms of democracy were irresistible in the modern world. Few modern thinkers have explicitly rejected it. 'Holistic' thinkers—among them nationalists, Stalinists, Fascists and others—have done so, counting (some) individuals as of less or no value in comparison with the whole of which they form a dispensable part. More interestingly, it can be argued with considerable plausibility that Utilitarianism implies a rejection of this idea, since its concern is to aggregate experiences of satisfaction or utility, no matter *whose* experiences they are: thus, it is committed to 'atomism' applied to the individual person and need be no 'respecter of persons' in its computations of utilities and dis-utilities.[5] (On the other hand, it is not clear that the eighteenth- and nineteenth-century Utilitarians drew this implication: consider, for instance, Bentham's principle that each individual is to count for one and only one). It is an idea which has, to say the least, been treated with differing degrees of seriousness. Some have been prepared to ignore it in the short run, or to qualify it by balancing it against other principles; others, from the Levellers to the anarchists, have derived from it the most immediate and egalitarian conclusions. (Bakunin wrote that 'a man only truly becomes a man when he respects and when he loves the humanity and liberty of all, and when his liberty and his humanity are in turn respected, loved, sustained and created by all'.)[6] Moreover, there is clearly room for infinite dispute about its practical implications.

[4] *Ibid.*, p. 100.
[5] I owe this idea to Derek Parfit.
[6] M. Bakunin, *Dieu et l'état* in *Oeuvres*, Paris, 1895, tome I, pp. 280–81.

It is central to the thought of Jean-Jacques Rousseau, who wrote that 'Man is too noble a being to serve simply as the instrument for others. . .',[7] and it is likewise central to Thomas Paine, who maintained that

Public good is not a term opposed to the good of individuals; on the contrary, it is the good of every individual collected. It is the good of all, because it is the good of every one: for as the public body is every individual collected, so the public good is the collected good of those individuals.[8]

It is enshrined in the American Declaration of Independence, in the Declaration of the Rights of Man and in the Universal Declaration of Human Rights adopted by the General Assembly of the United Nations in 1948, which begins by declaring its 'recognition of the inherent dignity and of the equal and inalienable rights of all members of the human family'.

This idea achieved its most impressive and systematic expression in the writings of Immanuel Kant, who asserted that 'man, and in general every rational being, *exists* as an end in himself, *not merely as a means* for arbitrary use by this or that will: he must in all his actions, whether they are directed to himself or to other rational beings, always be viewed *at the same time as an end*', Rational beings, he argued,

are called *persons* because their nature already marks them out as ends in themselves—that is, as something which ought not to be used merely as a means—and consequently imposes to that extent a limit on all arbitrary treatment of them (and is an object of reverence). Persons, therefore, are not merely subjective ends whose existence as an effect of our actions has a value *for us*: they are

[7] J.-J. Rousseau, *Julie, ou la Nouvelle Héloise* (1761) V, lettre 2, ed. D. Mornet, Paris, 1925, IV, p. 22.
[8] Quoted in Halévy, *op. cit.*, p. 188.

objective ends—that is, things whose existence is in itself an end, and indeed an end such that in its place we can put no other end to which they should serve *simply* as means; for unless this is so, nothing at all of *absolute* value would be found anywhere.

Kant saw this principle as an '*objective* principle' from which 'it must be possible to derive all laws for the will', and as entailing the practical imperative: '*Act in such a way that you always treat humanity, whether in your own person or in the person of any other, never simply as a means, but always at the same time as an end*'.[9] In his earlier, pre-critical writings Kant followed Rousseau in seeking to ground this idea in an innate, universal, natural sentiment ('a feeling which dwells in every human heart and which is more than mere pity and helpfulness . . . a feeling for the Beauty and Dignity of human nature'),[10] while in his later, critical writings he offered an (unsuccessful) transcendental proof.

Countless modern thinkers have maintained this idea, and defended it in different ways. In particular, the philosopher McTaggart argued for it in an essay entitled 'The Individualism of Value', the thesis of which is that nothing has value (that is, 'ultimate value—value as an end, not value as a means'), but 'conscious beings and their states'; in particular, 'the individual is an end, the society is only a means' and the State 'can have no value but as a means'. As for the attribution of ultimate value to the latter, it is 'fetish-worship': it 'would be as reasonable to worship a sewage pipe, which also possesses considerable value as a means'.[11]

[9] I. Kant, *The Moral Law* (1785), tr. and ed. H. J. Paton, 3rd ed., London, 1956, pp. 95–6.

[10] Quoted by P. Haezraki, 'The Concept of Man as End-in-Himself' in R. P. Wolff (ed.), *Kant: a Collection of Critical Essays*, London, 1968, p. 295.

[11] J. McT. E. McTaggart, 'The Individualism of Value' in *Philosophical Studies*, London, 1934, pp. 101, 108, 109.

In general, this idea of the dignity of the individual has the logical status of a moral (or religious) axiom which is basic, ultimate and overriding, offering a general justifying principle in moral argument.

CHAPTER 8

Autonomy

Distinct from this first idea is a second: the notion of *autonomy*, *or self-direction*, according to which an individual's thought and action is his own, and not determined by agencies or causes outside his control. In particular, an individual is autonomous (at the social level) to the degree to which he subjects the pressures and norms with which he is confronted to conscious and critical evaluation, and forms intentions and reaches practical decisions as the result of independent and rational reflection.

It seems that this idea was first clearly expressed (since Aristotle) by Saint Thomas Aquinas. According to the traditional medieval doctrine, the order of a superior, whether just or unjust, had to be obeyed; for Thomas it need not, if conscience forbade its execution. His argument was that 'everyone is bound to examine his own actions in the light of the knowledge which he has from God'.[1] As Ullmann has commented,

The general principle he advocated was that 'every man must act in consonance with reason'—'omnis enim homo debet secundum rationem agere'—a principle which persuasively demonstrates the

---

[1] St. Thomas Aquinas, *Quaestiones Disputatae de Veritate*, qu. 17, art. 4, quoted in Ullmann, *op. cit.*, p. 127.

advance in individual ethics and a principle which begins to assert
the autonomy of the individual in the moral sphere.[2]

In the religious sphere that autonomy was clearly evident in
Luther's argument: '. . . each and all of us are priests because we
all have the one faith, the one gospel, one and the same sacra-
ment; why then should we not be entitled to taste or test, and
to judge what is right or wrong in the faith?':[3] Luther, it has
been said, 'replaced the [collective] piety shaped by the Church
by the piety of the autonomous person'.[4] The idea of autonomy
was also evident in Calvin's stress on the individual's responsibility and in his teaching that men's consciences 'have to do,
not with men, but with God alone.'[5] Beyond the religious
sphere, it was widely proclaimed during the Renaissance, above
all by the humanists. Pico della Mirandola expressed it most
eloquently in the words he attributes to God in his *Oration on
the Dignity of Man*:

Finally the Best of Workmen decided that that to which nothing of
its very own could be given should be given, in composite fashion,
whatsoever had belonged individually to each and every thing . . .
and He spoke to him as follows: We have given thee, Adam, no
fixed seat, no form of thy very own, no gift peculiarly thine, that . . .
thou mayest . . . possess as thine own the seat, the form, the gifts
which thou thyself shalt desire. . . . In conformity with thy free
judgment in whose hands I have placed thee, thou are confined by
no bonds, and thou wilt fix the limits of thy nature for thyself. . . .

---

[2] *Ibid.*
[3] *Reformation Writings of Martin Luther*, ed. B. L. Woolf, London, 1952,
Vol. I, p. 120.
[4] F. Richter, *Martin Luther und Ignatius von Loyola*, Stuttgart-Degerloch,
1954, p. 213, cited in W. Stark, *The Sociology of Religion: A Study of Christen-
dom*. Vol. III: *The Universal Church*, London, 1967, p. 368.
[5] J. Calvin, *Institutes of the Christian Religion* (1536), IV, x, 5, tr. J. Allen,
Philadelphia, n.d., Vol. II, pp. 452–3.

Neither heavenly nor earthly, neither mortal nor immortal have
We made thee. Thou . . . art the moulder and the maker of thyself. . . . Thou canst grow downward into the lower natures which
are brutes. Thou canst again grow upward from the mind's reason
into the higher natures which are divine.[6]

In the social, and especially political, sphere, it was one of the
cardinal values of the Enlightenment—and the main target of
the latter's critics, who were horrified by the *philosophes'*
exaltation of the individual's private judgment (hence De
Maistre's castigation of 'political protestantism carried to the
most absolute individualism.')[7]

The two thinkers with whom the idea of autonomy finds its
most systematic exposition are Spinoza and, once more, Kant.
The distinction between freedom and servitude is basic to
Spinoza's thought, and his characteristic notion of freedom
involves the active exercise of the power of thought: a free
man is an active, self-determining, thinking being, and the
paradigm of freedom is internally-determined reasoning leading to self-evident truths. For Spinoza freedom is a very special
kind of autonomy and consists in 'the integration of all [a
man's] desires and aversions into a coherent policy, the policy
of developing his own powers of understanding, and of enjoy-
ing his active energies'.[8] Thus Part V of the *Ethics* is entitled
'Of the Power of the Understanding, or of Human Freedom'.

As for Kant, his third practical principle for the will was 'the
Idea *of the will of every rational being as a will which makes universal
law*', according to which

all maxims are repudiated which cannot accord with the will's own
enactment of universal law. The will is therefore not merely subject

[6] Quoted in Kristeller, *op. cit.*, pp. 100–1.

[7] *See above.* Chapter I.

[8] S. Hampshire, 'Spinoza and the Idea of Freedom', *Proceedings of the
British Academy*, XLVI (1960), p. 213.

to the law, but is so subject that it must be considered as also *making the law* for itself and precisely on this account as first of all subject to the law (of which it can regard itself as the author).

Kant argued that to 'the idea of freedom there is inseparably attached the concept of *autonomy*, and to this in turn the universal principle of morality' and that 'when we think of ourselves as free, we transfer ourselves into the intelligible world as members and recognize the autonomy of the will together with its consequence—morality'.[9]

Autonomy is closely related to and sometimes equivalent to what has been called 'positive' freedom or liberty, as advocated principally by thinkers influenced by rationalism. In his 'Two Concepts of Liberty', Sir Isaiah Berlin describes this sense of liberty as deriving from 'the wish on the part of the individual to be his own master':

I wish my life and decisions to depend on myself, not on external forces of whatever kind. I wish to be the instrument of my own, not other men's, acts of will. I wish to be a subject, not an object; to be moved by reasons, by conscious purposes, which are my own, not by causes which affect me, as it were, from outside. I wish to be somebody, not nobody; a doer—deciding, not being decided for, self-directed and not acted upon by external nature or by other men as if I were a thing, or an animal, or a slave incapable of playing a human role, that is, of conceiving goals and policies of my own and realising them. This is at least part of what I mean when I say that I am rational, and that it is my reason that distinguishes me as a human being from the rest of the world. [10]

The burden of Berlin's essay is to point to the ominous consequences that have flowed from historical misapplications and extensions of this view of freedom as autonomy or rational

[9] Kant, *op. cit.*, pp. 98–9, 120–1.
[10] I. Berlin, *Four Essays on Liberty*, Oxford, 1969, p. 131.

E

self-direction. Freedom in this sense can turn and has turned into servitude when the reference of the autonomous 'self' has shifted from the actual, empirical individual to his 'real' or 'higher' or 'rational' self, and thence to the collectivity of which he is a member: 'the self to be liberated is no longer the individual but the "social whole" ' and 'men, while submitting to the authority of oligarchs or dictators . . . claim that this in some sense liberates them'. The ' "higher" self duly became identified with institutions, churches, nations, races, states, classes, cultures, parties, and with vaguer entities, such as the general will, the common good, the enlightened forces of society, the vanguard of the most progressive class, Manifest Destiny.' In the course of this process, 'what had begun as a doctrine of freedom turned into a doctrine of authority and, at times, of oppression, and became the favoured weapon of despotism. . . .'[11] But this ominous progression is neither logically compelling nor in itself relevant to the consideration of the idea of the autonomy of the individual. All ideas can be put to evil uses.

In fact, autonomy is a value that has always been central to liberalism. Thus, in the nineteenth century, Mill and Tocqueville were at one in fearing the dangers of increasing conformity, of the degeneration of men into 'industrious sheep' and in the belief that 'in this age the mere example of non-conformity, the mere refusal to bend the knee to custom is itself a service'.[12] In our own day, a commitment to individual autonomy can be seen in all those, whether liberals or neo-marxists or anarchists, who are sensitive to the many forms of repression, alienation and manipulation that are prevalent in the increasingly bureaucratized and large-scale industrial societies of our time. Herbert Marcuse's *One Dimensional Man*

[11] *Ibid.*, pp. 158, xliv.

[12] *On Liberty* in *On Liberty and Considerations on Representative Government*, ed. R. B. McCallum, Blackwell, Oxford, 1946, p. 59.

and the writings of Erich Fromm, who sees man as 'dehuman-
ized' in market society, experiencing 'himself as a thing to be
employed successfully on the market' rather than 'as an active
agent, as the bearer of human powers',[13] are extended pleas for
the regaining of a fast-disappearing autonomy, as is much
recent writing on the left. The same concern can be seen to
have underlain David Riesman's much more sanguine *The
Lonely Crowd*, which characterizes the 'autonomous' as those
who are 'free to choose whether to conform or not' to the
behavioural norms of their society and are 'capable of tran-
scending their culture', and which claims that, despite massive
pressures towards conformism and adjustment, 'people may,
in what is left of their private lives, be nurturing newly critical
and creative standards'. For Riesman,

Modern industrial society has driven great numbers of people into
anomie, and produced a wan conformity in others, but the very
developments which have done this have also opened up hitherto
undreamed-of possibilities of autonomy.[14]

In itself, the idea of autonomy is neutral with respect to the
issue of whether or not morality is relative and, in particular,
to whether moral values are subject to individual choice.[15] For
Kant, a commitment to the value of autonomy was clearly
compatible with objective moral certainty (though this was so
at least in part because Kant's autonomous individuals were
'rational wills' into whom adherence to certain moral principles had already been built). On the other hand, autonomy
has often been held to be incompatible with most versions
of determinism: as Kant put it, '. . . to be independent of

[13] E. Fromm, *The Same Society*, Greenwich, Conn., 1965, p. 129.
[14] D. Riesman *et. al.*, *The Lonely Crowd* (New Haven, 1950), abridged
ed. (Anchor Books), Garden City, 1953, pp. 278, 282, 349, 295.
[15] See below, Chapter 15.

determination of causes in the sensible world (and this is what reason must always attribute to itself) is to be free'.[16] Spinoza's idea of freedom, however, seeks to reconcile autonomy and determinism. Autonomy can be regarded as a presupposition of morality as such, as with Kant, or of fully human activity, as with Spinoza. It has, as we have seen, been widely held as a moral value—a condition of the individual that should be increased or maximized (though some existentialists have seen it as a burden inherent in the human condition). It is a value central to the morality of modern Western civilization, and it is absent or understressed in others (such as many tribal moralities or that of orthodox communism in Eastern Europe today).

[16] Kant, *op. cit.*, p. 120.

CHAPTER 9

Privacy

The third unit-idea is the notion of *privacy*, of a private existence within a public world, an area within which the individual is or should be left alone by others and able to do and think whatever he chooses—to pursue his own good in his own way, as Mill put it.

This has often been called an essentially modern idea and said to have been largely absent from ancient civilizations and medieval Europe.[1] 'In ancient feeling', according to Hannah Arendt,

the privative trait of privacy, indicated in the word itself, was all-important; it meant literally a state of being deprived of something, and even of the highest and most human of man's capacities. A man who lived only a private life, who like the slave was not permitted to enter the public realm, or like the barbarian, had chosen not to establish such a realm, was not fully human. We no longer think primarily of deprivation when we use the word 'privacy', and this is partly due to the enormous enrichment of the private sphere through modern individualism (*sic*).

The private, on her view, was for the ancients the realm of necessity, as opposed to the realm of freedom, namely the

[1] Cf. M. Villey, *Leçons d'histoire de la philosophie du droit*, new ed., Paris, 1962.

political or public realm. Thus the 'private realm of the house-hold was the sphere where the necessities of life, of individual survival as well as of continuity of the species, were taken care of and guaranteed'. In this sphere man did not exist as a truly human being: hence 'the tremendous contempt held for it by antiquity'. She sees this conception of privacy as totally opposed to the modern view:

Not only would we not agree with the Greeks that a life spent in the privacy of 'one's own' (*idion*), outside the world of the common, is 'idiotic' by definition, or with the Romans to whom privacy offered but a temporary refuge from the business of the *res publica*; we call private today a sphere of intimacy whose beginnings we may be able to trace back to late Roman, though hardly to any period of Greek antiquity, but whose peculiar manifoldness and variety were certainly unknown to any period prior to the modern age.[2]

This is a commonly stated argument with respect to the ancient and medieval worlds. Yet, the Epicureans were concerned to find the means to achieve private satisfactions and a self-sufficient, quiet life, and advocated the individual's withdrawal from public life and politics. And, as Miss Arendt herself recognizes, there occurred among the Romans a 'full development of the life of hearth and family into an inner and private space', in which art and science flourished.[3] Saint Augustine's *Confessions* have justly been called a 'manifesto of the inner world':[4] its author confesses to 'Thou, my inmost Physician . . . what I am within; whither [other men's] eye, nor ear, nor understanding can reach', including those secret, subconscious parts of the soul 'which Thine eyes know, mine

[2] Hannah Arendt, *The Human Condition* (Anchor Books), Garden City, 1959, pp. 35, 42, 35. Cf. *ibid.*, Pt. II, Chs. 4–9.
[3] *Ibid.*, p. 54.
[4] P. Brown, *Augustine of Hippo*, London, 1967, p. 168. Cf. *ibid.*, Ch. 16.

do not'. In the *Confessions*, Augustine explores the complex and mysterious recesses of his inmost self and he found God 'more inward to me, than my most inward part'. 'Great is the power of memory', he writes,

a fearful thing, O my God, a deep and boundless manifoldness; and this thing is the mind, and this am I myself. What am I then, O my God? What nature am I? A life various and manifold, and exceeding immense. . . .[5]

And indeed the whole tradition of Christian mysticism represents a cultivation of the private or inner sphere, in which the individual achieves a *secret* knowledge of and communion with God. This tradition reached a high point with the mystics of the fourteenth century. Consider, for example, the English mystic Walter Hilton, whose *The Ladder of Perfection* consists in a detailed and practical manual of the devout life and of the ascetic preparations required for embarking on a life leading towards spiritual perfection. 'It is for a man', wrote Hilton,

to enter into himself and come to the knowledge of his own soul and its powers, its beauties and its blemishes . . . [he] must withdraw his mind from the love of all earthly creatures, from vain thoughts, and images of all sensible things, and from all self-love.[6]

The more deeply one was 'at rest from outward things', the more 'awake' one became to 'the knowledge of God and of inward things'. The inspiration of God was

a secret word, for it is hidden from all who love the world, and

---

[5] *The Confessions of St. Augustine*, tr. by E. B. Pusey (Everyman Library), London, 1926, X, ii, 4 (pp. 205, 206); X, xxxvii, 60 (p. 242); III, vi, 11 (p. 40); X, xvii, 26 (p. 219).

[6] Quoted in D. Knowles, *The English Mystical Tradition*, London, 1964, p. 106.

revealed to those who love Him. It is by this means that a pure soul readily catches the sound of His murmured words, by which He reveals His truth. For each truth received by grace, and received with inward delight and joy, is a secret murmur of God in the ear of a pure soul.[7]

Neverthleless, it is true that privacy in its modern sense—that is a sphere of thought and action that should be free from 'public' interference—does constitute what is perhaps the central idea of liberalism—though, as we have seen, Burckhardt found its origins in the Renaissance. Liberalism may be said largely to have been an argument about where the boundaries of this private sphere lie, according to what principles they are to be drawn, whence interference derives and how it is to be checked. It presupposes a picture of man to whom privacy is essential, even sacred, with a life of his own to live. Berlin has linked this idea with 'negative liberty', involving a 'sense of privacy . . . of the area of personal relationships as something sacred in its own right . . .', arguing that, for all its religious roots, it 'is scarcely older, in its developed state, than the Renaissance or the Reformation'. This, according to Berlin,

is liberty as it has been conceived by liberals in the modern world from the days of Erasmus (some would say of Occam) to our own. Every plea for civil liberties and individual rights, every protest against exploitation and humiliation, against the encroachment of public authority, or the mass hypnosis of custom or organized propaganda, springs from this individualistic, and much disputed, conception of man.[8]

We have already met this idea in Tocqueville who, though

[7] Walter Hilton, *The Ladder of Perfection*, tr. L. Sherley-Price (Penguin Books), London, 1957, pp. 228, 252. I am grateful to Jeremy Catto for drawing my attention to the writings of Hilton.

[8] Berlin, *op. cit.*, pp. 129, 127–8.

alarmed by the social and political consequences of the excessive
retreat into privacy under democracy, nevertheless held 'negative liberty' as a pre-eminent value. It is found (with different
conceptions of the private area free from interference) in
Locke, Paine, Burke, Jefferson and Acton. It is found, above
all, in the writings of John Stuart Mill and Benjamin Constant,
which contain the classical liberal justifications for preserving
private liberty.

For Mill,

The only part of the conduct of any one, for which he is amenable
to society, is that which concerns others. In the part which merely
concerns himself, his independence is, of right, absolute. Over himself, over his own body and mind, the individual is sovereign.

There is, Mill argued,

a sphere of action in which society, as distinguished from the individual, has, if any, only an indirect interest; comprehending all that
portion of a person's life and conduct which affects only himself, or
if it also affects others only with their free, voluntary, and un-
deceived consent and participation.

This, 'the appropriate region of human liberty', comprises,
first,

liberty of conscience in the most comprehensive sense; liberty of
thought and feeling; absolute freedom of opinion and sentiment on
all subjects, practical or speculative, scientific, moral or theological
[and] liberty of expressing and publishing opinions . . . ;

second,

liberty of tastes and pursuits; of framing the plan of our life to suit
our own character; of doing as we like, subject to such consequnces

as may follow: without impediment from our fellow-creatures, so long as what we do does not harm them, even though they should think our conduct foolish, perverse, or wrong;

and third, 'the liberty, within the same limits, of combination among individuals. . . . .' In general, Mill wrote, the

only freedom which deserves the name, is that of pursuing our own good in our own way, so long as we do not attempt to deprive others of theirs, or impede their efforts to obtain it.[9]

Constant, whom Berlin justly calls the 'most eloquent of all defenders of freedom and privacy',[10] likewise defended 'liberty in everything, in religion, in philosophy, in literature, in industry, in politics' against 'authority which would like to govern through despotism' and against 'the masses who claim the right to subject the minority to the majority'. For him,

everything which does not interfere with order; everything which belongs only to the inward nature of man, such as opinion; everything which, in the expression of opinion, does not harm others . . .; everything which, in regard to industry, allows the free exercise of rival industry—is individual and cannot legitimately be subjected to the power of society.[11]

Foreshadowing Hannah Arendt, Constant further remarked on the essentially modern character of this idea of liberty as 'the peaceful enjoyment of personal independence': the ancients, 'to preserve their political importance and their part in the administration of the State, were ready to renounce their private independence', whereas

[9] Mill, *On Liberty* in Mill, *op. cit.*, pp. 9, 10–11.

[10] Berlin, *op. cit.*, p. 126.

[11] B. Constant, *Mélanges de littérature et de politique* (1829), Préface, in *Oeuvres*, Paris, 1957, p. 801.

Nearly all the enjoyments of the moderns are in their private lives: the immense majority, forever excluded from power, necessarily take only a very passing interest in their public lives.[12]

The relation of this idea to the institution of private property is plain, and it has accordingly been attacked, along with the latter, by many historical varieties of socialism. It can also be seen as contrasting, not only with authoritarian doctrines, but also with that powerful tradition of thought, reaching back through Elton Mayo to Rousseau, which stresses community and social integration as a means of curing psychological ills, or of achieving political and social purposes, through attachment to groups, whether they are primary groups, work groups, professional associations, classes, parties, religious orders, corporations, city-states or nations.

It is that tradition which David Riesman attacks in his essay 'Individualism Reconsidered', in which he concludes that 'to hold that conformity with society is not only a necessity but also a duty' is to 'destroy that margin of freedom which gives life its savour and its endless possibility for advance'. 'We must', he argues, 'give every encouragement to people to develop their private selves—to escape from groupism—while realizing that, in many cases, they will use their freedom in unattractive or "idle" ways'.[13] Perhaps the most striking, and without question the most influential, contemporary opposition to the idea of privacy is to be found in the thought of Mao Tse-Tung. As Mao wrote in 'Combat Liberalism' (September 1937), liberalism 'is extremely harmful in a revolutionary collective . . . a corrosive which eats away unity, undermines cohesion, causes apathy and creates dissension'; it 'stems from

[12] B. Constant, *De l'Esprit de conquête* (1814) in *Oeuvres*, pp. 1010, 1011, 1013.

[13] D. Riesman, *Individualism Reconsidered* (Glencoe, Ill., 1954), abridged ed. (Anchor Books), Garden City, pp. 26, 27.

petty-bourgeois selfishness, it places personal interests first and the interests of the revolution second . . .'; it is 'negative and objectively has the effect of helping the enemy'. A Communist should subordinate 'his personal interests to those of the revolution', consolidate 'the collective life of the Party and strengthen the ties between the Party and masses' and 'be more concerned about the Party and masses than about any private person, and more concerned about others than about himself.[14]

In general the idea of privacy refers to a sphere that is not of proper concern to others. It implies a negative relation between the individual and some wider 'public', including the state—a relation of non-interference with, or non-intrusion into, some range of his thoughts and/or action. This condition may be achieved either by his withdrawal or by the 'public's' forbearance. Preserving this sphere is characteristically held by liberals to be desirable, either for its own sake as an ultimate value, or as a value to be weighed against other values, or else as a means to the realization of other values, such as that to be considered next.

[14] *Selected Works of Mao Tse-Tung*, Peking, 1965, Vol. II, pp. 32–3. Compare Lenin's words to Young Communists in 1920: 'We recognize nothing private. Our morality is entirely subordinate to the interests of the class struggle of the proletariat' (V. I. Lenin, *Collected Works*, Vol. 31, Moscow, 1966, pp. 291–2). The Fascist opposition to 'liberal' ideas of privacy was no less pronounced—as Gentile wrote in 1943: 'And so, nothing private, and no limits to state action' (G. Gentile, *Genesis and Structure of Society*, tr. by H. S. Harris, Urbana, Ill., 1960, p. 179). (Both cited in L. Schapiro, *Totalitarianism*, London, 1972, pp. 34–5).

CHAPTER 10

Self-Development

If the notion of privacy is, at least in its modern form, typically liberal, the notion of *self-development* is, as we have seen above,[1] typically Romantic in origin. This idea, and the phenomenon of self-cultivation to which it refers, may perhaps be traced back to the Italian Renaissance, as it was by Burckhardt, but it was most fully elaborated among the early German Romantics, with their stress on qualitative (as opposed to numerical) uniqueness and individuality. Certainly one can find pre-Romantic precursors, as with Goethe and Rousseau, whose *Confessions* begin with the words: '. . . I am made unlike anyone I have ever met; I will even venture to say that I am like no one in the whole world. I may be no better, but at least I am different'.[2]

It was, however, the Romantics who applied this idea to all spheres of thought, art and life; it is in this sense that one recent scholar has observed that 'it was the real innovation of the Romantics to turn individualism into a whole *Weltanschauung*, to systematize it —in so far as their irrationalism permitted any logical ordering of ideas into a cohesive philosophy'.[3] Hence Novalis could write, with questionable logic, that 'Only the

---

[1] In Chapter 2.

[2] J.-J. Rousseau, *Les Confessions* (1782), ed. P. Grosclaude, Paris, 1947, p 33.

[3] L. Furst, *Romanticism in Perspective*, London, 1969, p. 58.

individual is of interest, therefore all that is classical is not individual', and proclaim it to be 'the supreme task of human
development to take possession of one's transcendental self, to
be, as it were, the quintessential ego of one's ego'.[4] Hence
Friedrich Schlegel could maintain that

It is just his individuality that is the primary and eternal element in
man. To make a cult of the formation and development of this
individuality would be a kind of divine egotism,[5]

conceiving the artist as the supremely creative and self-affirming
being who is to ordinary men what man is to other creatures
on earth. And Schleiermacher describes how

it became clear to me that each man ought to represent humanity in
himself in his own different way, by his own special blending of its
elements, so that it should reveal itself in each special manner, and,
in the fulness of space and time, should become everything that can
emerge as something individual out of the depths of itself.[6]

The same idea is found in Wilhelm von Humboldt, for
whom the 'true end of man' was 'the highest and most harmonious development of his powers to a complete and consistent whole', whose 'highest ideal . . . of the co-existence of
human beings' consisted in 'a union in which each strives to
develop himself from his own inmost nature, and for his own
sake', and who concluded that

reason cannot desire for man any other condition than that in which each
individual not only enjoys the most absolute freedom of developing himself by his own energies, in his perfect individuality, but in which external
nature even is left unfashioned by any human agency, but only receives

---

[4] Quoted in *ibid.*, pp. 56, 65.   [5] Quoted in *ibid.*, p. 65.
[6] F. D. E. Schleiermacher, *Monologue of 1800*, quoted in Meinecke, *op.
cit.*, p. 425.

the impress given to it by each individual of himself and his own free will,
according to the measure of his wants and instincts, and restricted only by
the limits of his powers and his rights.

For Humboldt, 'that towards which every human being must
ceaselessly direct his efforts, and on which especially those who
design to influence their fellow men must ever keep their eyes,
is the *Individuality of Power and Development*'. For this there are
two requisites: 'freedom and variety of situations', the preconditions for 'originality'.[7]

We have already briefly considered the subsequent history
of this idea within Germany: it soon developed into a theory
of organic community, the term *'Individuelle'* shifted its
reference from persons to supra-personal forces, and individuality came to be predicated of the *Volk*, or the State. On
the other hand, it has in its individual form continued to be
attractive to artists and intellectuals of all kinds ever since
Byron and Goethe.[8]

Apart from this, it entered into the liberal tradition, especially
through John Stuart Mill, whose 'On Liberty' was directly
influenced by Humboldt. In his *Autobiography*, Mill stresses the
'single truth' running through that essay: 'the importance, to
man and society, of a large variety in types of character, and of
giving full freedom to human nature to expand itself in in-
numerable and conflicting directions', and refers, as well as to
Humboldt, to 'the doctrine of individuality, and the claim of
the moral nature to develop itself in its own way' pushed by 'a
whole school of German authors even to exaggeration', and to
Goethe who likewise appealed to 'the theory of the right and
duty of self-development'.[9] Mill's version of this idea is clearly

[7] W. von Humboldt, *The Sphere and Duties of Government* (written in
1791), tr. J. Coulthard, London, 1854, pp. 11, 15, 17–18, 13.

[8] *See* Koebner, 1934.

[9] J. S. Mill, *Autobiography* (1873), New York, paperback edition, 1960, pp.
177, 179.

and eloquently set forth in Chapter III of 'On Liberty' ('Of Individuality, as One of the Elements of Well-being'). 'Among the works of man', Mill writes, 'which human life is rightly employed in perfecting and beautifying, the first in importance surely is man himself'; human nature 'is . . . a tree, which requires to grow and develop itself on all sides, according to the tendency of the inward forces which make it a living thing'. In true Romantic vein, Mill insisted 'emphatically on the importance of genius, and the necessity of allowing it to unfold itself freely both in thought and in practice . . .', but he took a characteristically liberal view of the social preconditions for the development of individuality: there 'should be different experiments in living' and 'free scope should be given to varieties of character, short of injury to others; and . . . the worth of different modes of life should be proved practically, when anyone thinks fit to try them'.[10]

The Romantic idea of individuality also entered as a crucial element into the ethical basis of marxism. Marx's view of man is of a being with a wide range of creative potentialities, whose 'own self-realization exists as an inner necessity, a *need*'. In the truly human society of communism there will be 'a new manifestation of *human* powers and a new enrichment of the human being' when 'man appropriates his manifold being in an all-inclusive way, and thus is a whole man'; objects will 'then confirm and realize his individuality' and, 'through the objectively deployed wealth of the human being . . . the wealth of subjective *human* sensibility (a musical ear, an eye which is sensitive to the beauty of form, in short, senses which are capable of human satisfaction and which confirm themselves as human faculties) is cultivated or created'.[11] The 'detail

[10] Mill, *op. cit.*, pp. 52, 58, 50.

[11] K. Marx, *Economic and Philosophical Manuscripts of 1844* in *Karl Marx, Early Writings*, tr. and ed. T. B. Bottomore, London, 1963, pp. 165, 168, 159, 161.

worker of today . . . reduced to the mere fragment of a man'
will be replaced by 'the fully-developed individual, fit for a
variety of labour', for whom 'the different social functions he
performs are but so many modes of giving free scope to his
own natural and acquired powers.'[12] Marx shared the Romantic
view of the artist as the paradigm of the creative individual:
indeed, in communist society, 'the exclusive concentration of
artistic talent in particular individuals, and its suppression in the
broad mass' will cease, and there will be 'no painters but at
most people who engage in painting among other activities'.
Finally, as opposed to Mill, Marx's conception of self-development is essentially communal: 'Only in community with
others has each individual the means of cultivating his gifts in
all directions'; 'the individuals obtain their freedom in and
through their association'.[13] Communism is a form of social
organization which transcends that of 'personal independence,
based on dependence on *things*' and makes possible 'Free individuality, based on the universal development of individuals
and on their joint mastery over their communal, social productive powers and wealth. . . . '[14]

The notion of self-development thus specifies an ideal for the
lives of individuals—an ideal whose content varies with
different ideas of the *self* on a continuum from pure egoism to
strong communitarianism. It is either anti-social, with the
individual set apart from and hostile to society (as among some
of the early Romantics), or extra-social, when the individual
pursues his own path, free of social pressures (as with Mill)
or highly social, where the individual's self-development is
achieved through community with others (as with Marx, or

[12] K. Marx, *Capital*, Vol. I (1867), Moscow, 1954, Ch. XV, Sec. 9, p. 488.
[13] K. Marx and F. Engels, *The German Ideology* (1845), Moscow, 1964,
pp. 431–2, 91–2.
[14] K. Marx, *Grundrisse der Kritik der politischen Ökonomie* (written 1857–
1858), Berlin, 1953, p. 76.

F

Kropotkin).[15] In general, it has the status of an ultimate value, an end-in-itself: as Mill put it,

In proportion to the development of his individuality, each person becomes more valuable to himself, and is therefore capable of becoming more valuable to others.[16]

[15] For Kropotkin, in a society organized on anarchist principles and 'mutual aid', man would be 'enabled to obtain the full development of all his faculties, intellectual, artistic and moral, without being hampered by overwork for the monopolists, or by the servility and inertia of mind of the great number. He would then be able to reach full *individualisation*, which is not possible either under the present system of *individualism*, or under any system of State Socialism in the so-called Volkstaat. . . .' (article on 'Anarchism' in *Encyclopedia Britannica*, 14th edition, London and New York, 1929–30, Vol. I, p. 873).

[16] Gierke, tr. Barker, p. 56.

CHAPTER 11

The Abstract Individual

[handwritten marginalia: eg Rawls, Hobbes — presocial]

The fifth element of individualism has a different logical status from the first four: it specifies, not a value or an ideal, but rather a way of conceiving the individual (which is not, however, morally neutral). According to this conception, individuals are pictured abstractly as given, with given interests, wants, purposes, needs, etc.; while society and the state are pictured as sets of actual or possible social arrangements which respond more or less adequately to those individuals' requirements. Social and political rules and institutions are, on this view, regarded collectively as an artifice, a modifiable instrument, a means of fulfilling independently given individual objectives; the means and the end are distinct. The crucial point about this conception is that the relevant features of individuals determining the ends which social arrangements are held (actually or ideally) to fulfil, whether these features are called instincts, faculties, needs, desires, rights, etc., are assumed as given, independently of a social context. This givenness of fixed and invariant human psychological features leads to an *abstract* conception of the individual who is seen as merely the bearer of those features, which determine his behaviour, and specify his interests, needs and rights.

This is what Otto Gierke had in mind when he observed that 'the guiding thread of all speculation in the area of Natural Law was always, from first to last, individualism—an individualism steadily carried to its logical conclusion', so that, for all modern Natural Law theorists, from Hobbes to Kant, 'a previous sovereignty of the individual was the ultimate and only source of Group-authority' and 'the community was only an aggregate—a mere union, whether close or loose—of the wills and powers of individual persons'; all these thinkers agreed that 'all forms of social life were the creation of individuals' and 'could only be regarded as *means to individual objects*'.[1]

Louis Dumont has well characterized Gierke's thesis as follows:

For the moderns, under the influence of Christian and Stoic individualism, natural law, as opposed to positive law, does not involve social beings but individuals, i.e. men each of whom is self-sufficient, as made in the image of God and as the repository of reason. This is to say that, in the idea of jurists in the first place, first principles regarding the constitution of the State (and of society) have to be extracted, or deduced, from the inherent properties or qualities or man taken as an autonomous being independently of any social of political attachment. The state of nature is the state, logically prior to social and political life, in which only individual man is considered, and, logical priority blending into historical anteriority, the state of nature is the state in which men are supposed to have lived before the foundation of society or state. To deduce from this logical or hypothetical state of nature the principles of social and political life . . . is the task which the theorists of modern Natural Law have undertaken, and it is in doing so that they have laid the basis for the modern democratic State.[2]

Gierke was right to locate the hegemony of this idea between the middle of the seventeenth and the beginning of the nine-

[1] *Ibid.*, pp. 96, 106, 111.
[2] L. Dumont, 'The Modern Conception of the Individual: Notes on its genesis and that of concomitant institutions', *Contributions to Indian Sociology*, No. VIII (October 1965), pp. 29–30.

teenth centuries. It was intimately related to the social contract mode of argument (revived in our own day in the work of John Rawls), and, in general, to arguments concerning society based on the conception of man in the state of nature, though it can also be seen in a different form—an abstract notion of man in general—in the early Utilitarians and the classical economists. Needless to say, the (pre-social, trans-social or non-social) 'individuals' involved here—whether natural, or utilitarian or economic men—always turn out on inspection to be social, and indeed historically specific. 'Human nature' always in reality belongs to a particular kind of social man.

The most penetrating critical account of this idea in its historical context is given by Marx, for whom, on the contrary, it was axiomatic that '*man* is not an abstract being, squatting outside the world. Man is *the human world*, the state, society'.[3] The passage where Marx discusses it is worth quoting at length. He describes the picture of isolated individuals with which Adam Smith and David Ricardo begin ('insipid illusions of the eighteenth century') and Rousseau's ' "contrat social", which makes naturally independent individuals come in contact and have mutual intercourse by contract' as 'the fiction and only the aesthetic fiction of the small and great Robinsonades':

They are, moreover, the anticipation of 'bourgeois society', which had been in course of development since the sixteenth century and made gigantic strides towards maturity in the eighteenth. In this society of free competition the individual appears free from the bonds of nature, etc., which in former epochs of history made him a part of a definite, limited human conglomeration. To the prophets of the eighteenth century, on whose shoulders Smith and Ricardo are still standing, this eighteenth-century individual, constituting the joint product of the dissolution of the feudal form of society and of

[3] K. Marx, *Contribution to the Critique of Hegel's Philosophy of Right: Introduction* (1844) in *Early Writings*, p. 43.

the new forces of production which had developed since the sixteenth century, appears as an ideal whose existence belongs to the past; not as a result of history, but as its starting point.

Since that individual appeared to be in conformity with nature and corresponded to their conception of human nature, he was regarded not as a product of history, but of nature. This illusion has been characterisitic of every new epoch in the past. Steuart, who, as an aristocrat, stood more firmly on historical ground, contrary to the spirit of the eighteenth century, escaped this simplicity of view. The further back we go into history, the more the individual, and, therefore, the producing individual seems to depend on and constitute a part of a larger whole: at first it is, quite naturally, the family and the clan, which is but an enlarged family; later on, it is the community growing up in its different forms out of the clash and the amalgamation of clans. It is but in the eighteenth century, in 'bourgeois society', that the different forms of social union confront the individual as a mere means to his private ends, as an outward necessity. But the period in which this view of the isolated individual becomes prevalent, is the very one in which the interrelations of society (general from this point of view) have reached the highest state of development. Man is in the most literal sense of the word a *zoon politikon*, not only a social animal, but an animal which can develop into an individual only in society. Production by isolated individuals outside of society—something which might happen as an exception to a civilized man who by accident got into the wilderness and already dynamically possessed within himself the forces of society—is as great an absurdity as the idea of the development of language without individuals living together and talking to one another.[4]

This abstract way of conceiving the individual is most clear in Hobbes, for whom Leviathan, or the sovereign power, is an artificial contrivance constructed to satisfy the requirements

[4] K. Marx, *Introduction to the Critique of Political Economy* (written 1857) in *A Contribution to the Critique of Political Economy*, tr. N. I. Stone, Chicago, 1913, pp. 266–8.

(chief among them survival and security) of the component elements of society—'men as if but even now sprung out of the earth, and suddenly, like mushrooms, come to full maturity, without all kind of engagement to each other'.[5] As for Locke, as Bentham observed, 'Men according to his scheme come into the world full grown, and armed at all points like the fruit of the serpent's teeth sown by Cadmus at the corners of his cucumber patch'.[6] A similar view is found in very many eighteenth-century thinkers, especially in France. Even Rousseau, as Hegel and Marx observed, at times speaks in terms of abstract individuals, though the central thrust of his thought is incompatible with this; thus he writes of the Legislator transforming 'each individual, who is by himself a complete and solitary whole, into part of a greater whole from which he in a manner receives his life and being'.[7] Perhaps the most explicit and most characteristic eighteenth-century expression of the idea occurs in an article in Diderot's *Encyclopedia* by Turgot, who wrote:

The citizens have rights, rights that are sacred for the very body of society; the citizens exist independently of society; they form its necessary elements; and they only enter it in order to put themselves, with all their rights, under the protection of those very laws to which they sacrifice their liberty.[8]

The notion of the abstract individual formed a principal

[5] T. Hobbes, *De Cive* (1642) in *The English Works of Thomas Hobbes*, ed. Sir William Molesworth, London, 1839–44, Vol. II, p. 109.

[6] Quoted in Halévy, *op. cit.* (French edition), *La Formation du radicalisme philosophique*, Paris, 1901, Vol. I, App. III, p. 418.

[7] J.-J. Rousseau, *The Social Contract* (1762), tr. G. D. H. Cole (Everyman Library), London, 1913, p. 32.

[8] A. R. J. Turgot, article on 'Fondation (Politique et Droit Naturel)' in the *Encyclopédie, ou Dictionnaire raisonné des sciences, des arts et des métiers*, Paris, 1752–72, Vol. VII, p. 75.

target for a great number of nineteenth-century thinkers, many
of whom held it to be a typically narrow and superficial dogma
of the Enlightenment. Alternative, essentially social conceptions of the individual were advanced by counter-revolutionary
and Romantic conservatives in France, England and Germany,
by Hegel and Marx and their respective followers, by Saint-
Simon and his disciples, by Auguste Comte and the Positivists,
by sociologists and social psychologists, chief among them
Durkheim and the American pragmatist George Herbert Mead,
by German historicists and jurists, and by English Idealists. It is
what De Bonald had in mind when he wrote: 'Not only does
man not constitute society, but it is society that constitutes man,
that is, it forms him by social education . . .';[9] and it is what
F. H. Bradley meant when he wrote that 'the "individual"
apart from the community is an abstraction', and accused the
'individualist' of falsely maintaining that 'the community is the
sum of its parts, is made by the addition of parts; and the parts
are as real before the addition as after; [and that] the relations
they stand in do not make them what they are, but are acci-
dental, not essential, to their being. . . .' Man, for Bradley, 'is
a social being; he is real only because he is social . . .' and if we
abstract from him all those features which result from his social
context, he becomes 'a theoretical attempt to isolate what
cannot be isolated'.[10]

[9] L. de Bonald, *Théorie du pouvoir* (written 1796), *Oeuvres*, Paris, 1854,
Vol. I, p. 103.
[10] F. H. Bradley, 'My Station and its Duties' (1876) in *Ethical Studies*,
second edition, Oxford, 1927, pp. 173, 164, 174, 171.

CHAPTER 12

Political Individualism

Next there is a familiar set of ideas, central to classical liberalism, which may be collectively labelled *political individualism*.
Underlying them is a picture of society whose members (or
rather whose politically relevant members) are, precisely,
abstract individuals, as described above: the citizens, on this
view, constitute 'independent centers of consciousness',[1] they
are independent and rational beings, who are the sole generators of their own wants and preferences, and the best judges of
their own interests—which can be identified by consulting
them or observing what they desire and aim at. Among the
ideas comprising political individualism are, first, a view of
government as based on the (individually-given) consent of its
citizens—its authority or legitimacy deriving from that consent. In the social contract theories of the seventeenth and
eighteenth centuries, this consent was represented as pre-dating
the institution of government, whose authority it thereafter secured; nineteenth- and twentieth-century liberals have
abandoned this fiction for another, namely, that of the continuing consent registered in free elections. Second, and allied
to this, is a view of political representation as representation,
not of orders or estates or social functions or social classes, but
of individual interests. And third, there is a view of the purpose
of government as being confined to enabling individuals' wants

[1] Robert Paul Wolff, *The Poverty of Liberalism*, Boston, 1968, p. 142.

to be satisfied, individuals' interests to be pursued and individuals' rights to be protected, with a clear bias towards *laissez-faire* and against the idea that it might legitimately influence or alter their wants, interpret their interests for them or invade or abrogate their rights.[2]

These ideas have a number of sources. Though theories of consent are found both in ancient and medieval political thought, the more individualistic versions date from the contractarians, especially Hobbes, Locke and Rousseau, and reached their clearest expression in the Enlightenment. In the state of nature preceding the social contract all men are free and equal, and no man can exercise authority over another except by the latter's consent. Hobbes's contract was the product of self-interested individuals seeking to escape from the dangerous insecurity of the state of nature, and their self-interest furnished the continuing basis for order and political authority. As Hegel justly observed, Hobbes, unlike his predecessors, 'sought to derive the bond which holds the state together, that which gives the state its power, from principles which lie within us, which we recognize as our own'.[3] The consent embodied in Locke's contract was similarly a matter of a series of individual, rational choices, though he took much of the sting (and interest) out of this view by his doctrine of 'tacit consent', according to which individuals may be said to have consented to a government in any society subsequent to the supposed contract simply by owning property, or by 'lodging only for a week', by 'travelling freely on the highway' and indeed even by being 'within

[2] Compare Wolff's account of 'the methodological individualism of the classical liberal tradition' with the foregoing account of 'political individualism'. Wolff writes: 'According to that tradition, political society is (or ought to be— liberalism is similarly ambiguous) an association of self-determining individuals who concert their wills and collect their power in the state for mutually self-interested ends' (*ibid.*, p. 124).

[3] *Hegel's Lectures on the History of Philosophy*, tr. E. S. Haldane and F. H. Simson, London, 1892–6, Vol. III, p. 316.

the territories of that government'.[4] Rousseau may be said to have carried this view to its logical conclusion, seeing individuals in civil society as ideally engaged in a continuous process of creation of the laws to which they were, in turn, subject— the 'conventions' which 'form the basis of all legitimate authority among men'—and seeing the Sovereign as 'formed wholly of the individuals who compose it'.[5] The article on 'Authority' in the *Encyclopédie* gives perhaps the clearest eighteenth-century account of this ultra-individualist view of consent through social contract:

The prince derives from his subjects the authority he holds over them; and this authority is limited by the laws of nature and of the state. The laws of nature and of the state are the conditions under which they have or are supposed to have submitted themselves to his rule. One of these conditions is that, having no power or authority over them except by their choice and their consent, he can never use this authority to break the act of contract by which it has been conferred on him. . . .[6]

Nineteenth- and twentieth-century liberal democrats, though they abandoned the doctrine of the social contract, have continued to appeal to the notion of individually given consent as legitimating democratic government. But they have never succeeded in providing a criterion for the existence of such consent more satisfactory than participation in free elections. Moreover, even supposing such a criterion could be established, thinkers of this kind have never been prepared to draw the distinctly anarchistic conclusion that, to the extent that such

---

[4] J. Locke, *The Second Treatise of Civil Government* (1690) in *The Second Treatise of Civil Government and A Letter Concerning Toleration*, ed. with an introduction by J. W. Gough, Blackwell, Oxford, 1946, Ch. VIII, Sec. 119, p. 60.

[5] Rousseau, *op. cit.*, pp. 7, 14.

[6] *Encyclopédie*, Vol. I, p. 898.

consent is lacking, the government is to that extent illegitimate. For this kind of argument one must turn to an ultra-liberal thinker such as Henry David Thoreau who, in his celebrated essay on 'Civil Disobedience' asks: 'Must the citizen even for a moment, or in the least degree, resign his conscience to the legislator?' and answers:

I think that we should be men first, and subjects afterward. It is not desirable to cultivate a respect for the law, so much as for the right. The only obligation which I have a right to assume is to do at any time what I think right.

Starting from the classical American liberal, Jeffersonian view that 'That government is best which governs least', and the radical democratic idea 'government is only the mode which the people have chosen to execute their will', Thoreau drew the stark conclusion that when the state makes men 'agents of injustice', then they should themselves dissolve 'the union between themselves and the state'.[7]

The individualist view of political representation as the representation of individual interests dates from the early nineteenth century and was articulated most clearly by the Utilitarians. Society was made up of millions of individuals, each pursuing his own interests, seeking pleasure and avoiding pain. Once the political system was reformed on the basis of manhood suffrage, annual elections and the abolition of the powers of the monarchy and the House of Lords, the elected representatives in the legislature would act in such a way that the happiness of all would be maximized. 'It is indisputable', wrote James Mill, 'that the acts of men follow their will; that their will follows their desires; and that their desires are generated by their apprehensions of good or evil; in other

[7] H. D. Thoreau, 'Civil Disobedience' reprinted in I. L. Horowitz (ed.), *The Anarchists*, New York, 1964, pp. 313–14, 312, 314, 319.

words, by their interests'.[8] Once the parliamentary system was reformed as proposed, the legislative assembly would have an 'identity of interest' with 'the rest of the community'; otherwise, without the necessary reforms, the representatives would 'follow their [own] interest and produce Bad Government'.[9] In particular, frequent elections would prevent the growth of 'sinister interests'. Just as the free market was assumed to lead to maximum benefit for all, so also would the reformed political system (with electors and representatives all pursuing their individual interests) maximize the aggregate satisfaction of men's separate individual interests. The 'invisible hand' worked in politics, just as in economics.

Samuel Beer has well described the crucial role in nineteenth-century Liberal politics of the idea that political representation was of individuals, distinguishing that politics from what he calls 'Old Tory' and 'Old Whig' politics. 'The Liberals', he writes

gave a new stress in their political thought to the representation of individuals rather than corporate bodies, ranks, orders or 'interests'. In their politics, as in their economics, the source of action was (or ought to be) the rational, independent individual.[10]

Among the practical consequences of this idea were the development toward equal electoral districts, until in 1885 'the individual for the first time became the unit, and numerical equality ("one vote, one value") the master principle';[11] the Liberal stress on property as a qualification for the franchise (as the 'best rough index' of the individual's 'intelligence and good will');[12] and the increasing uniformity of the franchise. It was

[8] James Mill, *Essay on Government* (1828) repr. with introd. by E. Barker, Cambridge, 1937, p. 62.   [9] *Ibid.*, pp. 66, 34.
[10] S. H. Beer, *Modern British Politics*, London, 1965, p. 34.
[11] R. C. K. Ensor, quoted in *ibid.*, p. 34.   [12] *Ibid.*

not only in England that this individualist view of representation was influential. In America too it was of great importance, and was central, for example to the thought of Madison, with his great fear of 'faction'. 'Individuals', writes Beer, 'not interest groups or classes, were the basic units of his ideal polity'.[13]

Finally, the individualist view of the purpose of government as protecting individuals' rights and allowing them maximum scope to pursue their interests owes much to Locke, on the one hand, and to the Utilitarians, on the other. Lockean liberalism stresses a view of the government's role as *protector* of the life, liberty and property of its citizens—above all, their property. The Utilitarians, on the other hand, provided the rationale for the liberal view of government as holding the ring, as referee, nightwatchman or traffic-policeman, while individuals pursue, in harmonious competition, their several interests. The 'individuals' in question were, of course, above all the middle classes, but the ideology embodied in utilitarianism was framed in universal, not class, terms. Dicey, as we have seen, called it 'systematized individualism', observing that it 'corresponded to the best ideas of the English middle class' and sought 'to realize by means of effective legislation the political and social ideals set before himself by every intelligent merchant, tradesman, or artisan'.[14] Marx made the same point when he noted that the 'utility theory' is prejudiced in favour of the conditions of the bourgeoisie:

The complete subordination of all existing relations to the relation of utility, and its unconditional elevation to the sole content of all other relations, we find for the first time in Bentham, where, after the French Revolution and the development of large-scale industry, the bourgeoisie no longer appears as a special class, but

[13] Beer, *op. cit.*, p. 38.
[14] Dicey, 1962, pp. 175, 173, 175.

as the class whose conditions of existence are those of the whole society.[15]

The picture of society underlying political individualism *alteration s* contrasts with pictures of society found among conservatives, among socialists and among modern pluralist thinkers, as well as with that derviing from a sociological perspective. For the conservative, society is naturally hierarchical, whether the natural divisions are ranks or estates or classes, resulting, as Burke put it, in an 'habitual social discipline, in which the wiser, the more expert and the more opulent conduct, and by conducting enlighten and protect, the weaker, the less knowing, and the less provided with the goods of fortune'.[16] Men are not born free and equal, rational and independent, but into an extraordinarily rich and complex web of 'prescription' and 'prejudice', custom and tradition, which provide them with security and discipline and give meaning to their lives. For the socialist, above all the marxist, men are likewise seen as moulded by their social environment, entering, as Marx said, into 'definite relations that are indispensable and independent of their will'.[17] Central to these relations are the relations of production—relations of exploitation and domination within which mutually antagonistic classes with fundamentally incompatible interests confront one another. For non-marxist socialists the conflict of interests may be less irresolvable but the picture of individuals shaped and controlled by a class society is a distinctively socialist one. For the pluralist, society is rather to be seen as a basically harmonious network of groups, organizations and associations, which both influence and compete for the loyalties of individuals. Individuals move in the interstices

[15] Marx and Engels, *The German Ideology*, p. 453.

[16] E. Burke, 'Appeal from the Old to the New Whigs' (1791) in *The Works of Edmund Burke* (World's Classics), London, 1907, Vol. V, p. 100.

[17] K. Marx, 'Preface to *A Contribution to a Critique of Political Economy*' (1859) in Marx and Engels, *Selected Works*, Moscow, 1962, Vol. I, pp. 362–3.

of these overlapping groupings, which provide them with a plurality of role-definitions and attachments, while serving to prevent both a tyrannical domination of the individual by the state and the growth of an overriding and all-embracing conflict within society. A sociological perspective differs from the individualist picture in revealing all the manifold ways in which individuals are dependent on, indeed *constituted by*, the operation of social forces, by all the agencies of socialization and social control, by ecological, institutional and cultural factors, by influences ranging from the primary family group to the value system of society as a whole.

All of these views dispute as both naïve and mistaken the individualist picture of the individuals forming society as 'independent centres of consciousness', as by nature rational and free, as the sole generators of their own wants and preferences. Their consciousness is rather seen as (partially or wholly) socially determined and their wants and preferences as socially or culturally patterned. As for the view that men are the best judges of their own interests, that 'interests' are subjectively defined rather than objectively determined, this runs counter both to conservative and marxist ideas.[18] According to the former, men's interests are set by the requirements of a stable social order; according to the latter they are defined in objective, class terms, so that, in failing to become class-conscious, men fail to perceive and pursue their objective interests.

The individualist notion of consent to government is opposed by all those who are sensitive to the many ways and channels by means of which the legitimacy of government is secured. Conservatives, pluralists and many sociologists choose to call the basis for this legitimacy 'consensus', while marxists attribute it rather to the successful imposition and inculcation of ideology and false consciousness, or, as Gramsci would say,

---

[18] *See* Isaac D. Balbus, 'The Concept of Interest in Pluralist and Marxian Analysis', *Politics and Society*, 1, 2, (1971), pp. 151–77.

the cultural *hegemony* of the ruling class. The individualist view of representation contrasts with theories of representation which see sectional interests, whether local or functional, as the relevant units—local communities, estates, ranks, orders, in pre-modern politics, and, in our own day, functional, economic and vocational groups (seen as the relevant units by Guild Socialists, by pluralists in England, France and America and by Fascists) and, finally, classes. Indeed, for the marxist, a liberal-democratic representative system is itself a façade which hides the underlying class conflict in liberal capitalist society.[19] Finally, the individualist *laissez-faire* view of the purposes of government contrasts with all those political theories which contemplate a larger and more active role for government than the protection of individual rights and allowing maximum scope for the pursuit of personal interests. Such theories tend, in any case, to take a less narrow and more *social* view of the content of individual rights and interests, and they argue for a much more activist and interventionist state as being necessary for the securing of such rights (e.g. the right to work, or to a minimum wage) and for the promotion of such interests (e.g. in education and welfare) for all. Such theories go beyond individualism in regarding the State as having a crucial role to play in the achieving of social or communal goals which are distinct from the individual pursuit of private satisfactions.

[19] On different views of representation, *see* Beer, *op. cit.* and A. H. Birch, *Representation*, London, 1971.

G

CHAPTER 13

Economic Individualism

About *economic individualism* we may be more brief. At its simplest it is a belief in economic liberty. As a doctrine, it amounts to the justification of certain culturally specific patterns of behaviour (such as the systematic pursuit of profit maximization, and what Max Weber tendentiously called 'rational economic conduct'[1]) and of the institutions and procedures within which such behaviour has developed (which Weber lists as: a prevalent norm of rational capital accounting, the appropriation of all physical means of production by autonomous private industrial enterprises, a free market in labour and commodities, rational technology, calculable law, 'free labour' with workers compelled to sell their labour services on the market, and the commercialization of economic life[2]). Economic individualism implies a consequent presumption against economic regulation, whether by Church or State. H. M. Robertson provides a useful and accurate definition, as follows:

It is not true, as too many writers nowadays suggest, that the difference between the individualist scheme of life and the typical medieval or the typical socialist scheme of life is that the individualist has no social ideals while the others have. What is true is that the individualist has different ideals. Individualism, as a doctrine, sees

[1] Weber, *The Protestant Ethic*, p. 27.

[2] M. Weber, *General Economic History*, tr. F. H. Knight, London, 1923, pp. 207–9.

in the individual and his psychological aptitudes the necessary basis of society's economic organization, believes that the actions of individuals will suffice to provide the principles of society's economic organization, seeks to realize social progress through the individual by allowing him all the scope for his free self-development which is possible. It believes that for this two institutions are necessary: economic freedom (that is, freedom of enterprise) and private property. It believes that different individuals have different aptitudes and that each should be allowed to develop them in competition with others to the best of his ability. Therefore, as a system, individualism is the system of free trade, of competition, of private property.[3]

Ever since Max Weber and Werner Sombart, economic historians and sociologists have argued about when and how that system emerged in the West, and in particular about its relation to the various forms of Protestantism. It was, however, not until the mid-eighteenth century that its justification could make use of a coherent economic theory, with the work of Adam Smith and David Ricardo in Britain and the Physiocrats in late eighteenth-century France, with their view of the economy as a natural harmonious order. Henceforth economic individualism became both an economic theory and a normative doctrine, asserting (if so complex a tradition, or set of traditions, can be reduced to a formula) that a spontaneous economic system, based on private property, the market, and freedom of production, contract and exchange, and on the unfettered self-interest of individuals, tends to be more or less self-adjusting; and that it conduces to the maximum satisfaction of individuals and to (individual and social) progress.

In a sense, the whole history of (non-marxist) economics since Adam Smith can be seen as an ever-more sophisticated elaboration of the model of a competitive, private enterprise economy,

[3] H. M. Robertson, *Aspects of the Rise of Economic Individualism*, Cambridge, 1933, p. 34.

considered in abstraction from political and social factors. As one scholar has observed in relation to this model:

The welter of buying and selling that goes on in a division-of-labour economy is not a chaos. It is an orderly integrated system by which wants and productive efforts are meshed together, and the autonomous changes that occur in either are accommodated by a disciplined adjustment in the system of economic interdependencies.[4]

The fullest and clearest nineteenth-century models of such a system were developed by Léon Walras in his *Elements d'économie politique*, presenting it as a general equilibrium system, and by Alfred Marshall in his *Principles of Economics*. The increasingly complex and elegant neo-classical economic theories of this century are only further developments of this tradition.

On the other hand, not all these economic theorists have adopted the normative doctrine of economic *laissez-faire*. As Weber wrote, 'Pure economics is a theory which is "apolitical", which asserts "no moral evaluations", and which is "individualistic" in its orientation . . . The extreme free traders, however, conceived of it as an adequate picture of "natural" reality, i.e., reality not distorted by human stupidity, and they proceeded to set it up as a moral imperative—as a valid normative ideal—whereas it is only a convenient ideal type to be used in empirical analysisis'.[5] However, it can plausibly be argued that, despite its traditional claims to 'value freedom',

[4] H. Scott Gordon, 'Laissez-Faire' in *International Encyclopedia of the Social Sciences*, New York, 1968. I am indebted to this article for much of the material in this and the next two paragraphs.

[5] M. Weber, 'The Meaning of "Ethical Neutrality" in Sociology and Economics' (1917) in *Max Weber on the Methodology of the Social Sciences*, tr. and ed. by Edward Shils and H. A. Finch, Glencoe, Ill., 1949, p. 44.

economics (including present-day neo-classical economics) is inherently normative, tending to present the core institutions of capitalism—private property, the market, free competition, etc.—as meeting the requirements of efficiency and equity. This argument has been powerfully advanced by Gunnar Myrdal, who writes:

Even when the claim is not explicitly expressed, the conclusions unmistakably imply the notion that economic analysis is capable of yielding laws in the sense of *norms*, and not merely laws in the sense of *demonstrable recurrences and regularities of actual and possible events*.

Thus the theory of 'free competition' is not intended to be merely a scientific explanation of what course economic relations would take under certain specified assumptions. It simultaneously constitutes a kind of proof that these hypothetical conditions would result in maximum 'total income' or the greatest possible 'satisfaction of needs' in society as a whole. 'Free competition' thus on logical and factual grounds becomes more than a set of abstract assumptions, used as a tool in theoretical analysis of the causal relations of facts. It becomes a political *desideratum*.[6]

Strictly speaking, however, only those economists, politicians or publicists who seek to make reality conform to the model of a spontaneous, competitive, private enterprise economy are to be counted as adherents of economic individualism, which is essentially the view that the minimum of state interference and the maximum of economic liberty are both efficient and desirable. (Its rejection is perhaps a generic negative definition of 'socialism'—a term coined in the early 1830s in explicit opposition to its assumptions.)

Thus Adam Smith, though he was opposed to the manifold governmental restrictions on economic activity in his time, was not opposed to state intervention in the economy on principle;

[6] G. Myrdal, *The Political Element in the Development of Economic Theory*, tr. by P. Streeten, London, 1953.

and the classical economists in general favoured certain forms of state intervention (e.g. on matters such as sanitation, health and conditions of factory employment). Though mistrustful of state intervention, they were not doctrinaire believers in economic individualism in the strongest sense. For such views one must turn to publicists such as Harriet Martineau and the weekly London *Economist*, to the Liberal politicians who defended the poor law in the 1830s and opposed the growth of working men's combinations and state welfare provisions throughout the nineteenth century, and to theorists such as Herbert Spencer in England, Frédéric Bastiat in France and the Social Darwinists in America.

Perhaps the most systematic and sophisticated defenders of extreme economic individualism in our own day are economists such as Ludwig von Mises, Milton Friedman and F. A. Hayek, who sees it (that is, 'true individualism') as a matter of preserving those 'spontaneous formations which are the indispensable bases of a free civilization', in particular, an 'effectively competitive market', in the face of 'the present desire for comprehensive economic planning' and 'the basic view which wants all social activity to be recognizably part of a single coherent plan'.

This kind of view, descending as it does from the ascendant *laissez-faire* liberalism of the nineteenth century, represents a sort of defensive conservatism confronting welfare liberalism in the twentieth. It presents the vanishing ideal of an unregulated capitalism as an alternative to what are seen as the dangers of planning, bureaucratization and the implementation of redistributive and welfare policies by the government—all of which for Hayek are just steps along the 'road to serfdom'. 'Man in a complex society', he writes,

can have no choice but between adjusting himself to what to him must seem the blind forces of the social process and obeying the orders of a superior. So long as he knows only the hard discipline of the market, he may well think the direction by some other intelligent human brain preferable; but when he tries it, he soon discovers that the former still leaves him at least some choice, while the latter leaves him none, and that it is better to have a choice between several unpleasant alternatives than being coerced into one.[7]

Thus Friedman doubts that governments can manage their economies successfully and criticizes most social services as economically inefficient: instead he advocates a negative income tax and giving money to the poor.[8] Hayek advocates the abandonment of economic planning, the severe curbing of trade union powers, the dismantling of progressive taxation, the dropping of planning and rent controls, the withering away of the direct provision of education by the state, the restoration of wealth as a criterion for entry into higher education and the cessation of governmental conservationist policies.[9] These are the implications of present-day economic individualism at its strongest. They involve, not a policy of *laissez-faire*, but the demand that the government provide a framework within which competition and the price mechanism should be protected and promoted. In the context of monopoly capitalism, with giant corporations increasingly controlling markets and consumer behaviour, this demand becomes ever more anachronistic. Yet, as Myrdal's argument above suggests, it is a demand implicit in the mainstream of present-day orthodox neo-classical economics.

[7] Hayek, *Individualism and Economic Order*, pp. 25, 24.

[8] *See*, e.g., M. Friedman, *Capitalism and Freedom*, Chicago, 1963.

[9] *See* Hayek's writings, *passim*. On Hayek, *see* M. M. Wilhelm, 'The Political Thought of Friedrich A. Hayek', *Political Studies*, XX (1972), pp. 169–84 and J. C. Rees, 'Hayek on Liberty', *Philosophy*, XXXVIII (1963), pp. 346–60.

CHAPTER 14

Religious Individualism

Religious individualism may be defined as the view that the individual believer does not need intermediaries, that he has the primary responsibility for his own spiritual destiny, that he has the right and the duty to come to his own relationship with his God in his own way and by his own effort. Thus Troeltsch wrote of the 'emergence of religious individualism' along with the 'destruction of the old sociological organism of the sacramental and sacerdotal Church', a 'religious individualism which has no external organisation and which has a very independent attitude, with widely differing views of the central truths of Christianity', which 'is neither Church nor sect, and has neither the concrete sanctity of the institution nor the radical connection with the Bible'.[1] Indeed, Troeltsch claimed that 'the really permanent attainment of individualism was due to a religious and not a secular movement, to the Reformation and not the Renaissance'.[2]

Religious individualism is thus both a religious doctrine and, by implication, a view of the nature of religion; and it points to two further and important ideas: spiritual equality and religious self-scrutiny. The former had been stressed in the Early Church and the latter had been manifest in St. Augustine's *Confessions*. Indeed, religious individualism could be traced back at least to

[1] Troeltsch, *The Social Teaching of the Christian Churches*, Vol. I, p. 328.
[2] *Ibid.*, p. 381.

Jeremiah, but its modern forms characteristically date from the Reformation, when it was expressed in terms of the 'inner light', justification by faith and the universal priesthood of the believers.

It evidently embraces a wide range, from the most communal forms of Protestantism to cults of private mysticism, but it has usually, and rightly, been associated with Calvinism (despite the authoritarianism and intolerance of Calvinists when in power, as in Geneva, Scotland and Massachusetts). Here spiritual self-scrutiny and the 'internalization of conscience' were carried to their extremes: the Calvinists, in their pursuit of the certainty of being among the elect, engaged in the most ruthless self-examination and concentration on their own independent achievements.[3] This 'tended to make the individual increasingly egocentric, and it also produced a strained intensity in the pursuit of the utmost possible perfection'.[4] The individual's relation to God was direct and unmediated, and one of contract, or covenant: as opposed to the Catholic view of a relation between God and the whole of mankind, and of the collectivity of the Church as the mediator of redemption. It is this distinction which Werner Stark draws as follows:

Catholicism . . . is an incarnation of the principle which Tönnies called community: the whole is before the parts. Calvinism, on the other hand, is a product of the principle of association: the parts are before the whole. Catholicism thinks in terms of organic unity; it is collectivistic. Calvinism for its part thinks in terms of contractualism; it is individualistic.

Thus 'the Calvinist is the lonely man *par excellence* as the

[3] See I. Watt, *The Rise of the Novel: Studies in Defoe, Richardson and Fielding*, London, 1957, Ch. III for an examination of the literary consequences of Puritanism's interspective tendency.
[4] Troeltsch, *op. cit.*, Vol. II, p. 590.

Catholic is the archetypally sociable man . . . the great aim of the former is individual, and of the latter collective, sanctification'.[5] As Weber wrote, 'In spite of the necessity of membership in the true Church for salvation, the Calvinist's intercourse with his God was carried on in deep spiritual isolation'. Weber stresses the connection between the doctrine of predestination and 'a feeling of unprecedented loneliness of the single individual', given 'the complete elimination of salvation through the Church and the sacraments (which was in Lutheranism by no means developed to its final conclusion) . . .':

In what was for the man of the age of the Reformation the most important thing in life, his eternal salvation, he was forced to follow his path alone to meet a destiny which had been decreed for him from eternity.

This 'inner isolation of the individual', Weber argued, 'forms one of the roots of that disillusioned and pessimistically inclined individualism which can even today be identified in the national character and the institutions of the peoples with a Puritan past . . .'[6]

Since the Reformation, religious individualism has taken very many forms, the most extreme being that which bases religious certainty on the individual's act of faith. In the seventeenth century, Pascal presented such a fideistic conception of Christianity, picturing man as a poor and wretched creature, able to attain knowledge of first principles not by the use of reason, but by the heart. In his famous argument of the wager, Pascal sought to show that, in the absence of the possibility of rational proof, it was reasonable to gamble on the existence of God and seek religious guidance, since that choice offered the possibility of eternal life and happiness, and nothing

---

[5] W. Stark, *The Sociology of Religion*, Vol. III, pp. 251, 252.

[6] Weber, *The Protestant Ethic*, pp. 104–7.

would be lost if one were mistaken—'if you win, you win everything; if you lose, you lose nothing'. To remain an unbeliever in this situation was to take an infinitely unreasonable risk.[7]

Since Pascal, and often compared with him, the most profound and influential exponent of religious individualism has been Søren Kierkegaard, who wrote that 'if I were to desire an inscription for my tombstone, I should desire none other than "That Individual" '.[8] Kierkegaard, who may be considered the first existentialist, stood for a conception of Christianity as a personal private inward faith and he bitterly opposed what he saw as the falsifying conformism and worldliness of the Lutheran Church. The crowd, he wrote, 'regarded as a judge over ethical and religious matters, is untruth'. It is 'the untruth, by reason of the fact that it renders the individual completely impenitent and irresponsible, or at least weakens his sense of responsibility by reducing it to a fraction'. St. Paul's dictum that 'only one attains the goal' meant for Kierkegaard that

every man can be that one, God helping him therein—but only one attains the goal. And again this means that every man should be chary about having to do with 'the others', and essentially should talk only with God and with himself. . . .

The truth 'consists precisely in that conception of life which is expressed by the individual': it

can neither be communicated nor be received except as it were under God's eyes, not without God's help, not without God's being involved as the middle term, He himself being the Truth. It can

[7] *Pensées de Pascal*, ed. L. Bruschvicg, Paris, 1958, § 233.
[8] S. Kierkegaard, ' "That Individual": Two Notes concerning my Work as an Author' (1859) in *The Point of View*, tr. by W. Lowrie, London, 1939, p. 131.

therefore only be communicated by and received by 'the individual', which as a matter of fact can be every living man.[9]

'The Individual', he wrote, 'is the category through which, in a religious respect, this age, all history, the human race as a whole must pass' and Kierkegaard saw himself as standing 'in defence of this narrow defile', 'the individual' urging others to pass through it.[10] For Kierkegaard, man has the responsibility of making ultimate and undetermined choices, the supreme choice being whether or not to accept God's Word. In the most absolute possible sense, religious belief was for him a matter of individual choice and will. It is for these reasons that Kierkegaard can justly be characterized as standing 'at an extreme point, both in the development of Christianity and in the development of individualism'.[11]

[9] *Ibid.*, pp. 112–21.
[10] *Ibid.*, p. 130–2.
[11] Alasdair MacIntyre, *A Short History of Ethics*, London, 1967, p. 218.

CHAPTER 15

Ethical Individualism

Ethical individualism is a view of the nature of morality as essentially individual. In the seventeenth and eighteenth centuries this may be seen as having taken the form of ethical egoism, according to which the sole moral object of the individual's action is his own benefit. Thus the various versions of self-interest ethics, from Hobbes onwards, maintained that one should seek to secure one's own good, not that of society as a whole or of other individuals. Often, as with Hobbes, this doctrine was underpinned by another, which we may call 'psychological egoism', according to which men always act in their own interest, as Hobbes said, 'of the voluntary acts of every man, the object is some *good to himself*'.[1] But as often as not, this was not an empirical psychological doctrine, but rather a piece of conceptual legislation prescribing that all ostensible acts of altruism or benevolence are to be redescribed as really self-interested. Thus, for instance, pity for Hobbes 'is imagination or fiction of future calamity to ourselves, proceeding from the sense of another man's calamity'.[2] As Hume put it, a 'Hobbist' tries to 'explain every affection to be self-love, twisted and moulded, by a particular turn of imagination, into

---

[1] Hobbes, *Leviathan* in *The English Works of Thomas Hobbes*, Vol. III, p. 120.

[2] Hobbes, *The Elements of Law* in *ibid.*, Vol. IV, p. 44.

a variety of appearances'.[3] However, although psychological egoism entails ethical egoism (since if one cannot act except in one's own interest, then one's only moral obligation—given that 'ought' implies 'can'—would be so to act), the reverse is not true: not all ethical egoists have been psychological egoists.

Ethical egoism was most popular in the period between Hobbes and the early nineteenth-century Utilitarians—the problem always being to reconcile an ethic of self-interest with the requirements of social order and harmony. The most striking solution was that of Bernard Mandeville, whose men are driven by their private, self-seeking passions and yet, through 'the Happy contrivance of playing our Passions against one another', economic prosperity and social harmony can be achieved. In this way, 'Private Vices by the dextrous Management of a skilful Politician may be turn'd into Publick Benefits' and

> Thus every Part was full of Vice,
> Yet the whole Mass a Paradise.[4]

Others simply assumed a natural harmony of interests, while theologians such as Paley and Tucker argued that social co-operativeness is really conducive to long-term (that is, post-humous) self-interest. Finally, Bentham and other early Utilitarians seem for the most part to have assumed that pursuit of one's own happiness and that of the greatest number would either coincide or fail to conflict.

Ethical egoism is a doctrine which postulates the *object* of morality as exclusively individual, but there is a further

[3] D. Hume, *Enquiries Concerning The Human Understanding and Concerning The Principles of Morals*, ed. by L. A. Selby-Bigge, 2nd ed., Oxford, 1902, pp. 296–7.

[4] B. Mandeville, *The Fable of the Bees* (1724), edited with an introduction by Philip Harth (Penguin Books), London, 1970, pp. 167, 371, 67.

doctrine, which essentially dates from the nineteenth century, that we shall henceforth call 'ethical individualism' (as opposed to 'ethical egoism'). Indeed, if ethical egoism began with Hobbes and Mandeville and reached its height in the seventeenth and eighteenth centuries, ethical individualism can be said to have arisen in its most forceful and influential form with Kierkegaard and Nietzsche and to have achieved full expression in the nineteenth and twentieth centuries. According to this doctrine, the *source* of morality, of moral values and principles, the creator of the very criteria of moral evaluation, is the individual: he becomes the supreme arbiter of moral (and, by implication, other) values, the final moral authority in the most fundamental sense.[5]

The kinship between religious and ethical individualism in this sense is, it will be obvious, extremely close. Indeed, Kierkegaard's early work *Either/Or. A Fragment of Life* (1843) presents the choice between a life of pleasure-seeking and a life of duty as ultimately up to the individual, who, in making this choice, is bereft of any objective criterion not itself subject to choice, that would show one alternative superior to the other (though Kierkegaard himself evidently regarded the life of duty as superior). Moreover, ethical individualism can be seen as the philosophical consequence of taking the idea of autonomy seriously and carrying it to its logical conclusion. It was in this way that many thinkers derived ethically relativist conclusions from reading Kant: if man is autonomous, why should not the very choice of values, of the very criteria of evaluation, be up to him? Finally, ethical individualism is intimately linked with the view that facts and values are logically distinct, that no empirical description of the world compels us to adopt any particular set of moral evaluations or principles, or even limits the range of our possible value preferences. Rightly or wrongly,

[5] *See* A. Montefiore, 'Fact, Value and Ideology' in A. Montefiore and B. Williams (eds.), *British Analytical Philosophy*, London, 1966.

many philosophers have taken this view to derive from Hume, who, observing that all writers about morality moved without explanation from 'is' to 'ought', maintained that 'the distinction of vice and virtue is not founded merely on the relations of objects, nor is perceiv'd by reason' but arises, in his view, from 'feeling or sentiment', from 'perceptions in the mind'.[6] On the other hand, Hume did not see any problems arising from this position with regard to the relativity of morals, since he believed that all men had more or less the same moral sentiments or perceptions, for 'mankind is much the same in all times and places.'[7]

It could, indeed, be argued that ethical individualism is a position which can only be maintained by someone whose language embodies this distinction between fact and value, that is, a language whose moral vocabulary enables him to make statements which are distinctively either factual or evaluative. Utilitarianism, for example, provides such a vocabulary, as do contemporary uses of terms such as 'good' and 'bad'—as opposed to the moral vocabularies of earlier periods of our history or of other, less 'individualistic' cultures, where central moral terms such as 'chivalry', 'honour', 'piety' and so on are an intrinsic part of an established structure of roles and obligations and are in their contexts of use ineradicably both descriptive *and* evaluative.[8]

The rise of ethical individualism clearly has much to do with the decline of Christianity as an all-pervading basis for moral certainty. Some thinkers reacted to this situation by going

[6] D. Hume, *A Treatise of Human Nature*, ed. L. A. Selby-Bigge, Oxford, 1951, Bk. III, Pt. I, Sec. I, p. 469. Cf. A. MacIntyre, 'Hume on "Is" and "Ought"', *Philosophical Review*, 1959, reprinted in A. MacIntyre, *Against the Self-Images of the Age*, London, 1971.

[7] D. Hume, *Essays Moral and Political*, ed. T. H. Green and T. H. Grose, London, 1875, Vol II, p. 68.

[8] *See* MacIntyre, *A Short History of Ethics, passim.*

beyond ethical individualism to an extreme moral scepticism, beyond saying that individuals create their own moralities to saying that no moralities are true. As Nietzsche put it,

The end of Christianity—at the hands of its own morality (which cannot be replaced), which turns against the Christian God: the sense of truthfulness, highly developed by Christianity, is nauseated by the falseness and mendaciousness of all Christian interpretations of the world and of history; rebound from 'God is the truth' to the fanatical faith 'All is false'; an active Buddhism.

Scepticism regarding morality is what is decisive. The end of the moral interpretation of the world, which no longer has any sanction after it has tried to escape into some beyond, leads to nihilism. 'All lacks meaning'. . . .[9]

Nietzsche himself, however, sought to transcend this nihilism and, through a 'transvaluation of values', arrive at a new and higher form of morality, the morality embodied in the *Übermensch*.

The relation between the decline of religion and ethical individualism is revealed most clearly in the thought of Max Weber (which itself owed much to Nietzsche). For Weber,

The fate of our times is characterized by rationalization and intellectualization and, above all, by the 'disenchantment of the world'.

Men were 'destined to live in a godless and prophetless time' and were thus bereft of any revealed meaning to the world and to the conduct of life. Science could not provide such a meaning; the most it could achieve was *clarity* about what means are required to achieve a given end and about what the consequences of pursuing a given end are likely to be. The ends themselves are in irreconcilable conflict and ultimately subject

[9] F. Nietzsche, *The Will to Power*, Bk. I, tr. by W. Kaufmann in his *Existentialism from Dostoevsky to Sartre* (Meridian Books), New York, 1956, p. 110.

H

to individual choice. The 'ultimately possible attitudes towards life are irreconcilable, and hence their struggle can never be brought to a final conclusion. Thus it is necessary to make a decisive choice'. Weber gave the following example:

What man will take upon himself the attempt to 'refute scientifically' the ethic of the Sermon on the Mount? For instance, the sentence, 'resist no evil', or the image of turning the other cheek? And yet it is clear, in mundane perspective, that this is an ethic of undignified conduct; one has to choose between the religious dignity which this ethic confers and the dignity of manly conduct which preaches something quite different; 'resist evil—lest you be co-responsible for an overpowering evil'. According to our ultimate standpoint, the one is the devil and the other the God, and the individual has to decide which is God for him and which is the devil. And so it goes throughout all the orders of life.[10]

Among twentieth-century philosophies, existentialism, descending from Kierkegaard and Nietzsche, represents perhaps the most interesting and influential formulation of ethical individualism—though it has taken other forms, such as emotivism (as in the work of the American philosopher C. L. Stevenson)[11] and prescriptivism (represented by the contemporary Oxford moral philosopher, R. M. Hare[12]—for whom, as for Hume, 'mankind is much the same in all times and places'). As with Nietzsche and Weber, the existentialism of the early Sartre begins from the disappearance of religious certainty:

The existentialist . . . finds it extremely embarrassing that God does not exist, for there disappears with Him all possibility of finding

[10] 'Science as a Vocation' (1918) in *From Max Weber: Essays in Sociology*, ed. H. H. Gerth and C. W. Mills, London, 1948, pp. 155, 153, 152, 148.

[11] *See* esp. C. L. Stevenson, *Ethics and Language*, New Haven, 1944.

[12] *See* esp. R. M. Hare, *The Language of Morals*, Oxford, 1952 and *Freedom and Reason*, Oxford, 1963.

values in an intelligible heaven. There can no longer be any good *a priori*, since there is no infinite and perfect consciousness to think it. It is nowhere written that 'the good' exists, that one must be honest and not lie, since we are precise now upon the plane where there are only men. Dostoevsky once wrote 'If God did not exist everything would be permitted'; and that, for existentialism, is the starting point. Everything is indeed permitted if God does not exist, and man is in consequence forlorn, for he cannot find anything to depend upon either within or outside himself. He discovers forthwith, that he is without excuse. For if indeed existence precedes essence, one will never be able to explain one's action by reference to a given and specific human nature; in other words, there is no determinism—man is free, man is freedom. Nor, on the other hand, if God does not exist are we provided with any values or commands that could legitimize our behaviour. Thus we have neither behind us nor before us in a luminous realm of values, any means of justification or excuse. That is what I mean when I say that man is condemned to be free.

For Sartre, to follow existing moralities or to accept the advice of others as *authoritative* was bad faith, a denial of man's permanent and inescapable responsibility to *choose*. The individual cannot 'find help through some sign being vouchsafed upon earth for his orientation' for he 'himself interprets the sign as he chooses'. 'Man', he wrote,

makes himself; he is not found ready made; he makes himself by the choice of his morality, and he cannot but choose a morality, such is the pressure of circumstances upon him.

Existentialism was in this sense a humanism: it reminds man 'that there is no legislator but himself; that he himself, thus abandoned, must decide for himself'.[13] According to this stark

[13] J. P. Sartre, *Existentialism and Humanism*, tr. by Philip Mairet, London, 1948, pp. 33–4, 55–6.

doctrine (soon abandonned by Sartre), the view of the individual as source of morality reaches an extreme point—more extreme than with Kierkegaard—for there appears to be no limit either to his responsibility or to what he may count as moral.

It contrasts, as do all varieties of ethical individualism, with all objectivist or naturalistic ethical views, according to which the content of moral values and principles and the criteria governing moral judgements are not open to choice but are given—whether through revelation or reason or intuition or a proper understanding of the requirements of society or the direction of history or the principles of human nature. And indeed, strictly speaking, ethical individualism is also to be distinguished from any view of morality which, while allowing the individual a relative degree of choice between values and moral criteria, none the less sees limits to what can count as 'moral'. On such a view, certain principles and certain judgements (e.g. 'One ought to kill for pleasure') are simply outside the realm of morality in virtue of what morality is and of its role in human life. Perhaps the central unresolved problem of contemporary ethics is what degree of individual choice between ultimate values there is, and where the limits of morality are to be drawn. But, of course, to raise this very problem is implicitly to deny ethical individualism.

CHAPTER 16

Epistemological Individualism

Just as ethical individualism is a philosophical doctrine about the nature of morality, so *epistemological individualism* is a philosophical doctrine about the nature of knowledge, which asserts that the source of knowledge lies within the individual. Descartes' thought began from this position, from the individual's certainty of his own existence—*cogito ergo sum*—from which he derived knowledge of the external world and the past via the transcendental route of assuming God's veracity: Malebranche took a similar course. Again, Leibniz's metaphysics cannot be said to rest on an individualist epistemology, while Kant saw the categories as innate in the (abstract) *individual*. But the paradigm epistemological individualist is perhaps the empiricist, who holds that (individual) experience is the source of knowledge, that all knowledge arises within the circle of the individual mind and the sensations it receives.

This doctrine has taken a number of forms. For Locke, all the objects of thought are furnished by sense perception and consist in 'ideas'—whether ideas of sensation or ideas of reflection upon sensation, and whether simple or complex. All knowledge, he maintained, consists in *'the perception of the connection of and agreement, or disagreement and repugnancy, of any of our ideas'*[1]—which are caused in us by sensible things in the world.

[1] J. Locke, *An Essay concerning Human Understanding* (Everyman Library), London, 1947, Book IV, Ch. I, p. 252.

(On the other hand, Locke's epistemology in effect allowed for *a priori* knowledge—as of our own existence and that of God.) For Berkeley, sensible things have no existence outside the mind—their essence is to be perceived—and all knowledge (except for that of our own existence and of God) derives from sense perception. The individual is wholly enclosed within the circle of his mind, the ideas within it and its operations on those ideas: the certainty of his knowledge is assured by the fact that his sensations are by definition free from error. For Hume, no such assurance was possible, since his empiricism led him to scepticism about, for instance, the existence of the self or the external world (though in different ways and on different grounds in the two cases). For him, the contents of the mind were confined to 'impressions' given in perception, and 'ideas' —either simple ideas, which were copies of impressions, or complexes of such ideas. Knowledge is based either on the relations between ideas (as, for instance, in logic and mathematics) or on direct observation or experience. Finally among the traditional British empiricists, John Stuart Mill sought to account for our knowledge of the external world in terms of possibilities of sensation and even went so far as to claim that logical and mathematical knowledge was based on highly probable generalizations from experience.

Traditional empiricism was, in general, committed to a theory of psychological atomism, in which knowledge was seen as built up out of a mass of simple elements. As Hume said: 'Complex ideas may, perhaps, be well known by . . . an enumeration of those parts or simple ideas that compose them', themselves copies of 'impressions or original sentiments'.[2] In particular, the French disciples of Locke and Hume in the eighteenth century took this 'sensationalism' very seriously.

Twentieth-century empiricism, on the other hand, has, on the whole, been less concerned with the 'psychological'

[2] D. Hume, *Enquiries*, p. 62.

question of how knowledge is acquired than with the 'logical' question of what its 'basis' is, or how it may be validated. Here the central claim has been that all propositions whose truth is contingent (not logically necessary) and which we can know must be based on and reducible to propositions which directly report sense experience—'sense-datum propositions' which are basic and (for some) incorrigible. This is also, therefore, an atomistic kind of view (Bertrand Russell called an early version of it Logical Atomism) which sets itself the programme of building up the whole of our knowledge out of these elementary building blocks based on direct, individual experience —a programme now widely agreed to have been both unsuccessful and misdirected.

The crucial objection to empiricism, and to epistemological individualism generally, has taken two related forms: first, an appeal to a shared public world, and, second, to a shared, 'intersubjective' language, as preconditions or presuppositions of knowledge. The latter objection has become a commonplace of sociological and anthropological theory (receiving a classic statement in Durkheim's studies of primitive thought and religion) and of contemporary post-Wittgensteinian philosophy. Generally, epistemological individualism is to be contrasted with all those theories which hold that knowledge is, in part at least, the product of what Wittgenstein called 'forms of life' and is to be tested as genuine by reference to a public world.

CHAPTER 17

Methodological Individualism

Finally, we must examine a doctrine which has had an important place in the history of individualism, but which needs to be
very carefully analysed and distinguished from other doctrines
which have often been held either to entail it, or to be entailed
by it, or to be equivalent with it. Methodological individualism
is a doctrine about explanation which asserts that all attempts to
explain social (or individual) phenomena are to be rejected (or,
according to a current, more sophisticated version, rejected as
'rock-bottom' explanations) unless they are couched wholly in
terms of facts about individuals.

It was first clearly articulated by Hobbes, who held that 'it is
necessary that we know the things that are to be compounded,
before we can know the whole compound' for 'everything
is best understood by its constitutive causes',[1] the causes of the
social compound being Hobbesian men. It was taken up by the
thinkers of the Enlightenment, among whom, with a few
important exceptions (such as Vico and Montesquieu), an
individualist mode of explanation became pre-eminent,
though with wide divergences as to what was included, and in
particular how much of a social nature was included, in the
characterization of the explanatory elements. Man was seen by
some as egoistic, by others as co-operative. Some presupposed
the minimum about his social context in accounting for his
nature; others (such as Diderot) employed a genuine social

[1] *English Works of Thomas Hobbes*, Vol. I, p. 67; Vol. II, p. xiv.

psychology. Those who did the former, reasoning as though the 'individuals' in question were prior to society and undetermined by their social environment, were putting to work the abstract conception of the individual which we have considered above (in Chapter 11).

Methodological individualism was confronted, from the early nineteenth century onwards, by a wide range of thinkers who brought to the understanding of social life a perspective according to which collective phenomena were given priority over individuals in explanation. In France, this tradition passed from the theocrats, Saint-Simon and Comte (who wrote that a society was 'no more decomposable into *individuals* than a geometric surface is into lines, or a line into points')² through Espinas to Durkheim, whose whole sociology was founded on the denial of methodological individualism. In Germany this was a pervasive trend, encompassing all the social studies, such as history, economics, law, psychology, and philology. Both Marxists and Hegelians have likewise been committed to such a denial, as in the mainstream of modern sociology.

On the other hand, Max Weber was inclined to uphold it: as he wrote in a letter shortly before he died, '. . . . if I have become a sociologist . . . it is mainly in order to exorcize the spectre of collective conceptions which still lingers among us. In other words, sociology itself can only proceed from the actions of one or more separate individuals and must therefore adopt strictly individualistic methods'.³ Again, the Utilitarians

---

² A. Comte, *Système de politique positive*, Paris, 1851, Vol. II, p. 181.

³ Quoted in W. Mommsen, 'Max Weber's Political Sociology and his Philosophy of World History', *International Social Science Journal*, XVII (1965), p. 25. Fortunately, Weber did not systematically follow this methodological principle in his substantive sociological work. Consider, for example, his theory of stratification, based on structural rather than subjective factors; his account of the decline of the Roman Empire in terms of structural changes in Roman agriculture; and his explanation of the rationalization of the modern world in terms of such structural factors as the separation of the

were at one with John Stuart Mill in maintaining that 'the laws of the phenomena of society are, and can be, nothing but the actions and passions of human beings', namely, 'the laws of individual human nature'.[4] Many social scientists have been tempted to adopt methodological individualism, most obviously all those who have appealed to fixed psychological elements as ultimately explanatory factors—such as Pareto ('residues'), McDougall ('instincts'), Sumner ('drives'), and Malinowski ('needs')—and, notably, the sociologist George Homans.[5]

The debate over methodological individualism has recurred in many different guises—in the dispute between the German 'historical' school in economics and the 'abstract' theory of classical and neo-classical economics (especially as expounded by Carl Menger and the Austrian school), in endless disputes among philosophers of history and between sociologists and psychologists, and in the celebrated controversy between Durkheim and Gabriel Tarde (in which most of the basic issues were most clearly brought out).[6] Among others, Georg Simmel[7] and Charles Horton Cooley[8] tried to resolve the

household from the business enterprise. (*See* L. A. Coser, *Masters of Sociological Thought*, New York, 1971, p. 226).

[4] J. S. Mill, *A System of Logic*, 9th ed., London, 1875, Vol. II, p. 469. Men are not, Mill continues, 'when brought together converted into another kind of substance, with different properties' (*ibid.*).

[5] G. C. Homans, *The Nature of Social Science*, New York, 1968.

[6] *See* the present author's *Emile Durkheim*, London, 1973, Ch, 16, pp. 302–13.

[7] *See The Sociology of Georg Simmel*, tr. and ed. with introduction by K. H. Wolff, Glencoe, Ill., 1950, esp. Chs. I, II and V. (e.g. 'Let us grant for the moment that only individuals "really" exist. Even then only a false conception of science could infer from this "fact" that any knowledge which somehow aims at synthesising these individuals deals with merely speculative abstractions and unrealities', pp. 4–5).

[8] *See* C. H. Cooley, *Human Nature and the Social Order*, New York, 1912

dispute, as did Georges Gurvitch[9] and Morris Ginsberg,[10] but it constantly reappears, for example in the debate provoked by the polemical writings of Professors Hayek, Popper and Watkins in defence of methodological individualism, which we shall now briefly consider.[11]

For Cooley, society and the individual are merely 'the collective and distributive aspects of the same thing' (pp. 1–2).

[9] See G. Gurvitch, 'Les Faux Problèmes de la sociologie au XIXe siècle' in La Vocation actuelle de la sociologie, Paris, 1950, esp. pp. 25–37.

[10] See M. Ginsberg, 'The Individual and Society' in On the Diversity of Morals, London, 1956.

[11] See the following discussions: F. A. Hayek, The Counter-Revolution of Science, Glencoe, Ill., 1952, Chs. 4, 6 and 8; K. R. Popper, The Open Society and its Enemies, London, 1945 (4th. revised edition, 1962) ch. 14, and The Poverty of Historicism, London, 1957, chs. 7, 23, 24 and 31; J. W N. Watkins, 'Ideal Types and Historical Explanation', Brit. J. Phil. Sci., Vol. III (1952) (reprinted in H. Feigl and M. Brodbeck, Readings in the Philosophy of Science, New York, 1953); 'The Principle of Methodological Individualism' (note) ibid., Vol. III (1952); 'Historical Explanation in the Social Sciences', ibid., Vol. VIII (1957); M. Mandelbaum, 'Societal Laws', ibid., Vol. VIII (1957); L. J. Goldstein, 'The Two Theses of Methodological Individualism' (note), ibid., Vol. IX (1958); Watkins, 'The Two Theses of Methodological Individualism' (note), ibid., Vol. IX (1959); Goldstein, 'Mr Watkins on the Two Theses' (note), ibid., Vol. X (1959); Watkins, 'Third Reply to Mr. Goldstein' (note), ibid., Vol. X (1959); K. J. Scott, 'Methodological and Epistemological Individualism' (note), ibid., Vol. XI (1961); Mandelbaum, 'Societal Facts', Brit. J. Soc., Vol. VI (1955); E. Gellner, 'Explanations in History', Proc. Aristotelian Soc., supplementary Vol. XXX (1956). (These last two articles together with Watkins's 1957 article above are reprinted in P. Gardiner (ed.), Theories of History, Glencoe, Ill., 1959, together with a reply to Watkins by Gellner. Gellner's paper is here retitled 'Holism and Individualism in History and Sociology'); M. Brodbeck, 'Philosophy of the Social Sciences', Phil. Sci., Vol. XXI (1954); Watkins, 'Methodological Individualism: A Reply' (note), ibid., Vol. XXII (1955); Brodbeck, 'Methodological Individualisms: Definition and Reduction', ibid., Vol. XXV (1958); Goldstein, 'The Inadequacy of the Principle of Methodological Individualism', J. Phil., Vol. LIII (1956); Watkins, 'The Alleged Inadequacy of Methodological Individualism' (note), bid., Vol. LV (1958); C. Taylor, 'The Poverty of the Poverty of Historicism',

Hayek, for example, writes that

there is no other way toward an understanding of social phenomena but through our understanding of individual actions directed toward other people and guided by their expected behaviour.[12]

Similarly, according to Popper,

. . . all social phenomena, and especially the functioning of all social institutions, should always be understood as resulting from the decisions, actions, attitudes, etc., of human individuals, and . . . we should never be satisfied by an explanation in terms of so-called 'collectives' . . .[13]

Finally we may quote Watkins's account of 'the principle of methodological individualism':

According to this principle, the ultimate constituents of the social world are individual people who act more or less appropriately in the light of their dispositions and understanding of their situation. Every complex social situation, institution or event is the result of

Universities and Left Review, 1958 (Summer) followed by replies from I. Jarvie and Watkins, *ibid.*, 1959 (Spring); J. Agassi, 'Methodological Individualism', *Brit. J. Soc.*, Vol. XI (1960); E. Nagel, *The Structure of Science*, 1961, pp. 535–46; A. C. Danto, *Analytical Philosophy of History*, Cambridge, 1965, Ch. XII; W. H. Dray, 'Holism and Individualism in History and Social Science' in P. Edwards (ed.), *The Encyclopedia of Philosophy*, New York, 1967; S. Lukes, 'Methodological Individualism Reconsidered' (containing much of the contents of this chapter), *Brit. J. Soc.*, XIX (1968), pp. 119–29; J. O. Wisdom, 'Situational Individualism and the Emergent Group Properties', in R. Borger and F. Cioffi (eds.), *Explanation in the Behavioural Sciences*, Cambridge, 1970. For a useful summary of some points in this debate, *see* I. C. Jarvie, *Concepts and Society*, London, 1972, Appendix: 'The Methodological Individualism Debate'.

[12] Hayek, *Individualism and Economic Order*, p. 6.
[13] Popper, *The Open Society*, Vol. II, p. 98.

a particular configuration of individuals, their dispositions, situations, beliefs, and physical resources and environment. There may be unfinished or half-way explanations of large-scale social phenomena (say, inflation) in terms of other large-scale phenomena (say full employment); but we shall not have arrived at rock-bottom explanations of such large-scale phenomena until we have deduced an account of them from statements about the dispositions, beliefs, resources and inter-relations of individuals. (The individuals may remain anonymous and only typical dispositions etc., may be attributed to them). And just as mechanism is contrasted with the organicist idea of physical fields, so methodological individualism is contrasted with sociological holism or organicism. On this latter view, social systems constitute 'wholes' at least in the sense that some of their large-scale behaviour is governed by macro-laws which are essentially *sociological* in the sense that they are *sui generis* and not to be explained as mere regularities or tendencies resulting from the behaviour of interacting individuals. On the contrary, the behaviour of individuals should (according to sociological holism) be explained at least partly in terms of such laws (perhaps in conjunction with an account, first of individuals' roles within institutions, and secondly of the functions of institutions within the whole social system). If methodological individualism means that human beings are supposed to be the only moving agents in history, and if sociological holism means that some superhuman agents or factors are supposed to be at work in history, then these two alternatives are exhaustive.[14]

We can now turn to the task of distinguishing methodological individualism from a number of other, related theories, before analysing exactly what claims it advances. It has often, mistakenly, been taken to be the same as any or all of the following:

[14] Watkins, 'Historical Explanation in the Social Sciences', in P. Gardiner (ed.), *Theories of History* (see n. 11, p. 113), p. 505. Cf: 'Large-scale *social* phenomena must be accounted for by the situations, dispositions and beliefs of individuals. This I call methodological individualism' (Watkins, 'Methodological Individualism: A Reply', *Phil. Sci.*, Vol. XXII (1955) (see n. 11, p. 113), p. 58).

(1) A set of such purely truistic assertions as that society consists of people, that groups consist of people, that institutions consist of people who follow rules and fill roles, that traditions, customs, ideologies, kinship systems and languages are ways that people act, think and talk. These are truistic propositions because they are analytically true, in virtue of the meaning of words. Such a set of truisms has, of course, no implications as to the correct method of explaining social phenomena.

(2) A theory of meaning to the effect that every statement about social phenomena is either a statement about individual human beings or else it is unintelligible and therefore not a statement at all. This theory entails that all predicates which range over social phenomena are definable in terms of predicates which range only over individual phenomena and that all statements about social phenomena are translatable without loss of meaning into statements that are wholly about individuals. As Jarvie has put it, ' "Army" is merely a plural of soldier and *all* statements about the Army can be reduced to statements about the particular soldiers comprising the Army'.[15]

It is worth noticing that this theory is only plausible on a crude verificationist theory of meaning (to the effect that the meaning of p is what confirms the truth of p). Otherwise, although statements about armies are true only in virtue of the fact that other statements about soldiers are true, the former are not equivalent in meaning to the latter, nor *a fortiori* are they 'about' the subject of the latter.

(3) A theory of ontology to the effect that in the social world only individuals are real. This usually carries the correlative doctrine that social phenomena are constructions of the mind and 'do not exist in reality'. Thus Hayek writes, 'The social sciences . . . do not deal with "given" wholes but their task is to constitute these wholes by constructing models from the

[15] Jarvie, reply to Taylor (see n. 11, p. 114), p. 57.

familiar elements—models which reproduce the structure of relationships between some of the many phenomena which we always simultaneously observe in real life. This is no less true of the popular concepts of social wholes which are represented by the terms current in ordinary language; they too refer to mental models. . . .'[16] Similarly, Popper holds that 'social entities such as institutions or associations' are 'abstract models constructed to interpret certain selected abstract relations between individuals'.[17]

If this theory means that in the social world only individuals are observable, it is evidently false. Some social phenomena simply can be observed (as both trees and forests can); and indeed, many features of social phenomena are observable (e.g. the procedure of a court) while many features of individuals are not (e.g. intentions). Both individual and social phenomena have observable and non-observable features. If it means that individual phenomena are easy to understand, while social phenomena are not (which is Hayek's view), this is highly implausible: compare the procedure of the court with the motives of the criminal. If the theory means that individuals exist independently of, e.g., groups and institutions, this is also false, since, just as facts about social phenomena are contingent upon facts about individuals, the reverse is also true. Thus, we can only speak of soldiers because we can speak of armies: only if certain statements are true of armies are others true of soldiers. If the theory means that all social phenomena are fictional and all individual phenomena are factual, that would entail that all assertions about social phenomena are false, or else neither true nor false, which is absurd. Finally, the theory may mean that only facts about individuals are explanatory, which alone would make this theory equivalent to methodological individualism.

[16] Hayek, *The Counter-Revolution of Science*, p. 56.
[17] Popper, *The Poverty of Historicism* (paperback ed. 1961), p. 140.

(4) A negative theory to the effect that sociological laws are impossible, or that law-like statements about social phenomena are always false. Hayek and Popper sometimes seem to believe this, but Watkins clearly repudiates it, asserting merely that such statements form part of 'half-way' as opposed to 'rock-bottom' explanations.

This theory, however, is clearly unacceptable—since not all law-like statements about social phenomena are false—as Popper himself recognizes.[18]

(5) A doctrine which (ambiguously) asserts that society has as its end the good of individuals. When unpacked, this doctrine can be taken to mean any or all of the following: (a) that social institutions are to be explained as founded and maintained by individuals to fulfil their ends, framed independently of the institutions (as in, e.g., social contract theory); (b) that social institutions in fact satisfy individual ends; and (c) that social institutions ought to satisfy individual ends. (b) is typically held by economic individualists, such as Hayek, with respect to the market; (c) is typically held by political individualists who advocate a non-interventionist state on this ground, but neither (b) nor (c) either entails or is entailed by methodological individualism, whereas (a) is a version of it.

What, then, does methodological individualism claim? Briefly, we can say that it advances a range of different claims in accordance with how much of 'society' is built into the supposedly explanatory 'individuals'. Consider the following examples:

(i) genetic make-up; brain-states; condition of central nervous system

(ii) aggression; gratification; stimulus-response

(iii) co-operation; power; esteem

(iv) cashing cheques; saluting; voting

What this exceedingly rudimentary list shows is at least this:

[18] *See ibid.*, pp. 62–3.

that there is a continuum of what I shall henceforth call individual predicates from what one might call the most non-social
to the most social. Propositions incorporating only predicates
of type (i) are about human beings *qua* material objects and
make no reference to and presuppose nothing about consciousness or any feature of any social group or institution. Propositions incorporating only individual predicates of type (ii)
presuppose consciousness but still make no reference to and
presuppose nothing about any feature of any social grop uor
institution. Propositions incorporating only individual predicates of type (iii) do have a minimal social reference: they
presuppose a social context in which certain actions, social
relations and/or mental states are picked out and given a
particular significance (which makes social relations of certain
sorts count as 'cooperative', which makes certain social positions
count as positions of 'power' and a certain set of attitudes
count as 'esteem'). They still do not presuppose or entail any
particular propositions about any particular form of group or
institution. Finally, propositions incorporating only individual
predicates of type (iv) are maximally social, in that they presuppose and sometimes directly entail propositions about
particular types of group and institution. ('Voting Conservative'
is at an even further point along the continuum.)

Methodological individualism can be seen to have confined
its favoured explanations to any or all of these sorts of individual
predicates. We may distinguish the following four possibilities: (i) Attempts to explain in terms of type (i) predicates. The
most celebrated eighteenth-century example of this kind of
attempt is that made by the French materialist philosopher La
Mettrie, author of *L'Homme machine*, who sought to demon-
strate that the soul was physically or organically conditioned
and that its faculties and activities were causally dependent on
the central nervous system and the brain. The best contemporary example is the work of H. J. Eysenck. In his *The*

I

Psychology of Politics, Eysenck writes that: 'Political actions are actions of human beings; the study of the direct cause of these actions is the field of the study of psychology. All other social sciences deal with variables which affect political action indirectly'.[19] (Compare this with Durkheim's famous statement that 'every time that a social phenomenon is directly explained by a psychological phenomenon, we may be sure that the explanation is false').[20] In this book, Eysenck sets out to classify attitudes along two dimensions—the Radical-Conservative and the Tough-minded-Tender-minded—on the basis of evidence elicited by questionnaires. Then, having classified the attitudes, his aim is to *explain* them by reference to antecedent conditions —in particular the modifications of the individual's central nervous system, in abstraction from the 'historical, economic, sociological, and perhaps even anthropological context'.[21]

(ii) Attempts to explain in terms of type (ii) predicates. Examples here are Hobbes's appeal to appetites and aversions, Pareto's 'residues' and those Freudian and other theories in which the sexual or aggressive instinct is seen as generating a type of undifferentiated activity that is (subsequently) channelled in particular social directions, or else repressed or sublimated.

(iii) Attempts to explain in terms of type (iii) predicates. Examples are those sociologists and social psychologists who favour explanations in terms of general and 'elementary' forms of social behaviour, which do invoke some minimal social reference, but are unspecific as to any particular form of group, institution, or society. It was in this way that Tarde sought to account for much of social life in terms of the process of 'imitation' and it is in this way too that George Homans attempts to use the principles of Skinnerian-type psychology

[19] H. J. Eysenck, *The Psychology of Politics*, London, 1954, p. 10.
[20] É. Durkheim, *The Rules of Sociological Method*, New York, 1964, p. 104.   [21] Eysenck, *op. cit.*, p. 8.

and the terminology of 'costs' and 'rewards', arguing that 'within institutions', which differ greatly from society to society, 'in the face to face relations between individuals . . . characteristics of behaviour appear in which mankind gives away its lost unity'.[22]

(iv) Attempts to explain in terms of type (iv) predicates. Examples of these are extremely widespread and comprise all those cases where features of concrete, un-abstracted, specifically-located individuals are invoked in explanations—as, for instance when an election result is explained in terms of voters' motivations. Here, the relevant features of the social context (e.g., the class structure and the party system) are, so to speak, incorporated into the characterization of the individuals (as, e.g., working-class deferential Conservatives). If one opens any empirical work of sociology, or of history, explanations of this sort leap to the eye.

This, then, is the range of types of explanation prescribed by methodological individualism. An attack on methodological individualism involves showing that these types of explanation are either implausible or unpromising or question-begging. I would certainly wish to claim that types (i) and (ii) are highly implausible and unpromising ways of approaching the explanation of social phenomena, that type (iii) is very partial and cannot account for the differences between institutions and societies, and that type (iv) is question-begging, because it builds crucial social factors or features of society into the allegedly explanatory individuals (that is, in order to explain working-class Conservatism, we need to look at the class structure and at the party system).[23] Thus the social phenomena have not

[22] G. C. Homans, *Social Behaviour: its Elementary Forms*, London, 1961, p. 6.

[23] For a good example of just such a structural, sociological explanation, *see* F. Parkin, 'Working Class Conservatives', *Brit. J. Soc.*, XVIII (1967), pp. 278–90.

really been eliminated; they have been swept under the carpet.

Methodological individualism is thus an exclusivist, prescriptive doctrine about what explanations are to look like. In the first three forms considered above, it excludes explanations which appeal to social forces, structural features of society, institutional factors, and so on, while in the fourth form, it only appears to exclude such an appeal.

scale —
degrees
of methodological
individualism

PART THREE

The Relations between these Ideas

Ideas have natural affinities for one another, though what seems natural varies from age to age. It has often been claimed that the ideas and doctrines distinguished above are naturally related, that to be committed to one is to be committed to some, most or all of the others. This suggestion is clearly implicit in the passage from Halévy with which this book began. Though many individual thinkers have upheld some of these ideas while rejecting others, it has long been supposed that there are connections that are more than merely historical and contingent between humanist and liberal values, a view of society as a combination of (abstract) individuals, political and economic liberalism, protestantism, an individualist view of morals, empiricism and methodological individualism.

This has been supposed both by those who adhere to these ideas and by those who oppose them. For example, among liberals, many, from Locke to Bertrand Russell, have believed that there was an inherent connection between liberalism in morals and politics and an empiricist theory of knowledge, while others such as Weber (but see note 3, pp. 111–12), Hayek and Popper, have seen it as a matter of moral and political importance to defend methodological individualism. The ideology of contemporary conservatism in America combines political, economic and religious individualism: 'Americanism', it has been said, 'means individualism, *laisser-faire* and Christianity, usually of the fundamentalist Protestant type'.[1] Likewise, anti-individualists have also seen these various ideas as inseparably related. As Lévi-Strauss has observed,

The individualistic point of view of the eighteenth-century philosophers had been criticized by the theoreticians of reactionary thought, especially de Bonald, on the ground that social phenomena, having a reality *sui generis*, are not simply a combination of individual ones. There is a tradition linking individualism to humanism, while the assumption of the specificity of the collective in relation to the individual seems, also traditionally, to imply the higher value of the former over the latter.[2]

Culturally, it has been said, 'holism is intimately connected with hostility towards the liberal political individualism of the Western tradition'.[3] Conversely, anti-liberal thinkers on both left and right have been inclined to attack as 'individualism' an indistinct amalgam which comprises moral humanitarianism, an abstract view of 'the individual', the politics of liberal democracy and the economics of *laissez-faire* capitalism, protestantism and empiricism.

There are, clearly, interesting and complex relations of a logical or conceptual kind between some of these ideas and doctrines. In the following three chapters, we shall attempt to unravel some of these connections.

[1] M. M. Goldsmith and Michael Hawkins, 'The New American Conservatism', *Political Studies*, XX (1972), p. 71.

[2] C. Lévi-Strauss, 'French Sociology' in G. Gurvitch and W. E. Moore, (eds.), *Twentieth Century Sociology*, New York, 1945, p. 529.

[3] M. Brodbeck, 'Methodological Individualisms: Definition and Reduction' (see n. 11, p. 113), p. 3.

CHAPTER 18

Equality and Liberty

Our two cardinal ideals are called equality and liberty
LOUIS DUMONT[1]

The argument of this chapter is that the first four unit-ideas of individualism singled out above—respect for human dignity, autonomy, privacy and self-development—are essential elements in the ideas of equality and liberty; and specifically, that the idea of human dignity or respect for persons lies at the heart of the idea of equality, while autonomy, privacy and self-development represent the three faces of liberty or freedom. I shall further argue that these four basic ideas are, logically and conceptually, intimately interrelated.

My first claim is that the principle of respect for persons, as 'ends in themselves', in virtue of their inherent dignity as individuals, is at the basis of the ideal of human equality. What does this principle amount to? It amounts to the contention that all persons are deserving of respect, and should be treated accordingly. I shall say something below about what being a 'person' means in this context and what treatment with 'respect' consists in. What is worth stressing here is that this principle is strongly egalitarian, since it asserts that respect is *equally* due to all persons—in virtue of their being persons, that is of some

[1] L. Dumont, *Homo Hierarchicus: The Caste System and Its Implications*, tr. by Mark Sainsbury, London, 1970, p. 4.

characteristic or set of characteristics which they have in common—and since, as I shall argue, respecting them involves doing all one can to maintain and increase their freedom (and to discriminate between them in this regard is to fail to show them equal respect). Thus respecting persons contrasts with, for instance, praising or admiring them, for we distribute praise and admiration unequally. This is necessarily so, since we praise or admire people for characteristics which single them out from others. We praise someone for his particular achievements and we admire someone for his particular qualities or excellences; whereas we *respect* him *as a human being*, in virtue of characteristics which he shares with all other human beings. It might be objected that, since individuals may possess these characteristics to different degrees, they are therefore persons to different degrees. But to this it may be replied that it is the existence of the characteristics, not the degree to which they are possessed or actualized, which elicits the respect. There are, of course, differing accounts of what these characteristics are. The Christian ground for equal respect is that all men are equally children of God, while the Kantian argument is that they all have free and rational wills and are members of the Kingdom of Ends. Some have suggested that there are empirical features which all human beings share which provide grounds for treating them with equal respect—a suggestion we will consider below. The important point to note here, however, is that, whatever the grounds, the principle that they should be respected as persons implies that they should be *equally* so respected. It is a principle that has been at the heart of the ideal of equality from early Christianity to the present day—though it has often come into conflict with other moral and political principles, including another component principle of the ideal of equality, namely that of equality of opportunity (for, as Bernard Williams puts it, 'the idea of equality of respect is one which urges us to give less consideration to those structures in which people enjoy status or prestige, and to consider people independently of those goods, on the distribution of which equality of opportunity precisely focuses our, and their, attention').[2] Indeed, it is arguable that the principle of equality of opportunity (as opposed to equality of respect) rests on an abstract conception of the 'individuals' whose opportunities are to be equalized, imputing to them a certain range of self-interested and competitive wants and interests.

My second claim is that the notion of liberty or freedom is a complex or compound idea which, when subjected to analysis, can be shown to require or presuppose a number of further, more basic ideas, and that central to these are the notions of autonomy, privacy and self-development. Indeed, I would go further and claim that these can be seen, so to speak, as the 'three faces of freedom'—by which I mean that, while distinct from one another, all three are basic to the idea of freedom and that freedom is incomplete when any one of them is absent or diminished.

Consider the question: 'when is a person free?' I suggest that there appear to be at least three fundamental answers to this question, each of which is an indispensable part of the correct answer.

The first is that a person is free in so far as his actions are his own, that is, in so far as they result from decisions and choices which he makes as a free agent, rather than as the instrument or object of another's will or as the result of external or internal forces independent of his will. His autonomy consists precisely in this self-determined deciding and choosing. That autonomy is reduced in so far as his actions

[2] Bernard Williams, 'The Idea of Equality', in P. Laslett and W. G. Runciman (eds.), *Philosophy, Politics and Society* (*Second Series*), Blackwell, Oxford, pp. 129–30.

are determined elsewhere than by his conscious 'self'. Specifying when a person is acting autonomously is, of course, deeply problematic. There are clear cases of non-autonomy, as when someone is coerced or manipulated; but how are we to judge whether the person who conforms to the will of others or to the norms of his culture or the requirements of his role is doing so autonomously? A crucial element here is clearly that of consciousness and critical reflection. No less important is that the decisions and choices should be genuine ones—that there should be real alternatives between which the individual makes a choice (and that these alternatives should not be so loaded that he could not reasonably choose otherwise than he does). Thus the degree of his autonomy is a function, at least, of the degree of his self-consciousness and of the range of alternatives before him. His autonomy will be reduced to the extent that he is unaware of the determinants of his behaviour and to the extent that the alternatives before him are restricted. These are difficult and obscure issues, requiring much analysis. But what seems clear is that a person is free to the degree that he acts autonomously—and to the extent that his autonomy is reduced, so is his freedom.

A second answer to the question: 'when is a person free?' is that he is free when he is free *from* interferences and obstacles, and this is so to the extent to which he is left alone by others to think and act as he pleases. This is the so-called negative sense of freedom, which I prefer to see as an *aspect of* freedom, namely that which concerns what the individual is free *from*. Here we wish to stress, especially in political contexts, that a person is free *from* whatever might interfere with his doing what he wants or might want to do—with the proviso that the interference must be the result of human agency or of conditions which are seen as subject to human control. As Berlin writes, the 'extent of my social or political freedom [in this sense] consists in the absence of obstacles not merely to my actual, but to my potential choices—to my acting in this or that way if I choose to do so. Similarly absence of such freedom is due to the closing of such doors or failure to open them, as a result, intended or unintended, of alterable human practices, of the operation of human agencies'.[3] Underlying this conception is the notion of a sphere of thought and action within which the individual can claim the right not to be interfered with—and this area we may characterize as 'private' (without, however, the implication that it includes only thoughts and actions which concern himself alone). As Berlin, again, writes,

it is assumed, especially by such libertarians as Locke and Mill in England, and Constant and Tocqueville in France, that there ought to exist a certain minimum area of personal freedom which must on no account be violated; for if it is overstepped, the individual will find himself in an area too narrow for even that minimum development of his natural faculties which alone makes it possible to pursue, and even to conceive, the various ends which men hold good or right or sacred. It follows that a frontier must be drawn between the area of private life and that of public authority.[4]

Where that frontier is to be drawn and on what grounds can be and has been widely debated. But I suggest that some such minimum 'private' area, free from 'public' interference, is an essential component of the ideal of liberty. (Moreover, there is an 'inner' domain, integral to the self or personality, interference with which, as in hypnotism, is *necessarily* an invasion of freedom.) A person is free to the degree that this area is preserved—and to the extent that it is invaded, his freedom is diminished.

A third answer to the question: 'when is a person free?' is that a man is free to the extent to which he is able to shape his life's course and thereby realize his potentialities, that is, to make

[3] Berlin, *Four Essays on Liberty*, p. xl.   [4] *Ibid.*, p. 124.

out of himself the best of what he has it in him to be. This is what T. H. Green meant when he wrote that 'the ideal of true freedom is the maximum of power for all members of human society alike to make the best of themselves'.[5] This is a problematic conception, since there is the thorny problem of identifying what are to count as human 'potentialities', what it is for men to make 'the best of themselves'. There is a teleological component in this idea, a view of the true ends of man—with, of course, the attendant danger that those in power may defend the politically-controlled inculcation and development of certain desired capacities in their subjects as the true realization of their freedom, independently of the latter's wishes and aims. But this is merely a monstrous perversion of a valid, indeed essential component of the idea of individual freedom—namely the notion of self-development. Crucial to this idea are two constitutive elements: first, that it should be *self*-development— that I should as far as possible determine and control the course of my life; and second, that it should be self-*development*—that I should have the opportunity to bring to fruition certain characteristic human excellences. There is clearly much room for dispute about what these excellences are, whether a fully-human man must be many-sided or not, what self-development may be taken to rule out, and so on. And indeed, for the consistent ethical relativist there is the insurmountable difficulty that what counts as human excellence will be a matter of irresolvable moral disagreement. Nevertheless, my claim is that the opportunity to achieve self-development is an essential aspect of the ideal of human freedom. A person is free to the extent to which he is able to realize his human potentialities— and to the extent to which this self-realization is prevented (by humanly controllable factors), to that extent he is unfree.

[5] T. H. Green, 'Liberal Legislation and the Freedom of Contract' in *Works of Thomas Hill Green*, ed. R. L. Nettleship, London, 1885-8, Vol. III, p. 372.

Hence I conclude that equality is centrally based on human respect, and that liberty is an amalgam of personal autonomy, lack of public interference and the power of self-development.

I shall now argue that these ideas are intimately interrelated, logically and conceptually.

Let us first ask: what does 'respect for persons' really mean in practice and what does it rule out? This can be broken down into two distinct questions: first, in virtue of what characteristics do we accord respect to persons? and second, what does respecting them consist in?

What, then, are the distinguishing characteristics of persons on the basis of which we accord them dignity and respect? Another way of asking this is to ask what are the relevant features of human beings which mark them out as *persons* in the context of moral judgement? I have already suggested that Christians answer this question in religious terms, while Kant's transcendental answer has been called metaphysical. But it is arguable that these answers point implicitly to a number of empirical features which all human beings share, in virtue of which we regard them as persons and worthy of respect. Moreover, these are features which have been stressed by moralists and moral philosophers in varying degrees and with varying emphases throughout the ages.

The first such feature is the capacity of human beings to form intentions and purposes, to become aware of alternatives and make choices between them, and to acquire control over their own behaviour by becoming conscious of the forces determining it, both internally, as with repressed or subconscious desires and motives, and externally, as with the pressures exerted by the norms they follow or the roles they fill. In other words, human beings have the capacity to act autonomously, to become (relatively) self-determining, to become conscious of the forces determining or affecting them, and either to submit to them, recognizing their necessity, or to become independent of them. Obviously, not all men exercise this capacity to an equal degree, but all, except the mentally defective or deranged, possess it.

In the second place, human beings have the capacity to think thoughts, to perform actions, to develop involvements and to engage in relationships to which they attach value but which require a certain area of non-interference in order to have that value. Intellectual activities, artistic creation, love, friendship are examples: all these may be said to require a private space free of public interference or surveillance in order to flourish (though they may also be impaired by private interference). There is, of course, considerable room for differences about which of these human activities and relationships are of most value and about what kind of value they have, and indeed about which of them people should be left alone to engage in. Some may regard religious worship as paramount and sacrosanct; others may see the acquisition of wealth in this light. What seems indisputable is that there is a range of such activities and relations in some of which all persons have the capacity to engage and to which they attach value.

In the third place, human beings have the capacity for self-development—though, as we have seen, there are difficulties concerning how this is to be interpreted. It seems most satisfactory to understand it in the following way: that everyone has the capacity to develop in himself some characteristic human excellence or excellences—whether intellectual, aesthetic or moral, whether theoretical or practical, whether personal or public, and so on. Obviously, not everyone will be able to develop any given excellence to the same degree—and perhaps, *contra* Marx, not all will be able to develop them in a many-sided, all-round fashion. But all human beings share the capacity to realize potentialities that are worthy of admiration. What counts as worthy of admiration may be subject to moral disagreement and cultural variation, but my case is that there

is a delimited range of human excellences which are intrinsic-
ally admirable (though, of course, the forms they take will
differ from society to society) and that all human beings are
capable of achieving some of them to some degree.

I have argued that these three characteristics of persons—the
capacity for autonomous choice and action, the capacity to
engage in valued activities and relations that require a private
space, and the capacity for self-development—are at least part
of the ground on which we accord them respect. What, then,
does that respect consist in? My answer is that, whatever else it
involves, respecting persons involves treating them as (actually
or potentially) autonomous, as requiring privacy, and as
capable of self-development.

What, we may ask, constitutes a denial of such respect? We
cease to respect someone when we fail to treat him as an agent
and a chooser, as a self from which actions and choices emanate,
when we see him and consequently treat him not as a person
but as merely the bearer of a title or the player of a role, or as
merely a means of securing a certain end, or, worst of all, as
merely an object. We deny his status as an autonomous person
when we allow our attitudes to him to be dictated solely by
some contingent and socially defined attribute of him, such as
his place in the social order or his occupational role. Indeed, a
man may fail to respect himself in this sense, as in Sartre's
famous case of the waiter who comes to see himself merely as
the waiter playing a role, rather than as a person capable of
choice at every point in time.[6] There are other ways of deny-
ing someone's autonomy and thereby failing to respect him.
One way is simply to control or dominate his will; another is
unreasonably to restrict the range of alternatives between
which he can choose; but perhaps the most insidious and

---

[6] J. P. Sartre, *Existential Psychoanalysis*, tr. by Hazel Barnes, reprinted in
W. Kaufmann (ed.), *Existentialism, from Dostoevsky to Sartre* (Meridian Books),
New York, 1956, pp. 255 sqq.

decisive way is to diminish, or restrict the opportunity to increase, his consciousness of his situation and his activities.

Secondly, one manifestly fails to respect someone if one invades his private space and interferes, without good reason, with his valued activities (or, above all, with his inner self). Examples of where it can be justifiable so to interfere are in the cases say, of imprisonment, or conscription during wartime. In these and other cases, it may be claimed that there is 'good reason' for interference and thus no denial of respect in so far as they are necessary infringements of a person's freedom, either to preserve and enhance the freedom of others, or his own and others' in the long term, or as the only way of realizing other cherished values. But in the absence of these justifications, such an invasion or interference is clearly a denial of human respect. Consider, for example, the extreme forms of such a denial to be found in prison camps as described by Solzhenitsyn or total institutions as described by Erving Goffman.

Finally, I claim that one also importantly fails to respect someone if one limits or restricts his opportunities to realize his capacities of self-development. This may be done in various ways and in various contexts. It is the systematic and cumulative denial of such opportunities, in these various contexts, to the less favoured citizens of stratified societies, both capitalist and state socialist, that constitutes the strongest argument against the structured inequalities they exhibit. In the context of socialization, for example, such restrictions of opportunities are a central—one might even say, the central—topic studied by contemporary educational sociologists. A stratified educational system which reinforces other social inequalities and thereby blocks the self-development of the less favoured constitutes a denial of respect to persons (assuming, obviously, that the implied educational changes are amenable to political control). Similarly, to take another example, if it is possible to make certain types of work more challenging and require a greater development of talent or skill or responsibility, it is a denial of human respect to confine workers within menial, one-sided and tedious tasks. Furthermore, workers—and citizens in political society as a whole—are denied respect to the degree to which they are denied possibilities of real participation in the formulation and taking of major decisions affecting them, for they are thereby denied the opportunity to develop the human excellence of active self-government celebrated by Rousseau and J. S. Mill, and central to the various forms of classical democratic theory.

I have so far suggested that the notion of respect for persons has close conceptual relations with the ideas of autonomy, privacy and self-development: that it presupposes them as being among the grounds for such respect, and indeed that they are centrally involved in giving an account of what such respect *is*. I now wish to suggest that these three constituent ideas of freedom are themselves closely interrelated.

First, as Riesman argues, the exercise of autonomy requires a certain area of privacy or non-intervention by others: one cannot be self-determining if one's valued activities are constantly being interfered with (though what counts as 'interference' will depend in part on one's conception of the autonomous 'self'. Perhaps arranged marriages only become an 'interference' when the choice of a marriage partner enters the latter's orbit. On the other hand, as we have seen, we may also want to say that private freedom is invaded when certain alternatives are prevented from being conceived). Again, one central form of autonomy is precisely the autonomy to develop one's potentialities. Indeed, it could be argued that for John Stuart Mill, developing the capacity for choice through its continuous exercise precisely was the central form of self-development.[7]

[7] See Berlin, 'John Stuart Mill and the Ends of Life'—one of his *Four Essays on Liberty*.

K

Secondly, to talk of private freedom and 'negative liberty' logically implies autonomy: recall that Berlin's definition of the latter is in terms of obstacles to actual and potential *choices*. To the extent to which one's actions are not self-determined, the issue of not interfering with them becomes redundant; indeed, to the extent to which one's behaviour has been determined by others it has, in a quixotic sense, already been 'interfered with'. This is shown most clearly in cases of the manipulation of consciousness, such as hypnosis: the man under hypnosis can have no privacy and preventing him from doing some act suggested by the hypnotist is no invasion of his negative liberty (though it might be said to invade that of the hypnotist). Privacy, in the sense I have been using it, also involves self-development, to the degree to which the valued activities that are to be protected against public interference are activities which lead to self-development. As Berlin observes, a 'minimum area of personal freedom' is required for 'that minimum development of [the individual's] natural faculties which alone make it possible to pursue, and even to conceive, the various ends which men hold good or right or sacred.'[8]

Finally, self-development, as I have already suggested, presupposes autonomy. The very idea of *self*-development logically implies that the development is autonomously pursued —though clearly its course can be substantially assisted by providing the appropriate conditions and encouragements. Moreover, it is evident that many forms of self-development will require a certain private area of non-interference. One may, for example, be unable to develop creative artistic powers when one is constantly being told what and how to paint (though counter-examples—such as the Renaissance—spring to mind). Perhaps the strongest case is that of the effects of censorship on the development of intellectual virtues. (On the other hand, it can equally well be argued that certain forms of self-develop-

[8] Berlin, 'Two Concepts of Liberty' in *ibid.*, p. 124.

ment—such as that resulting from political participation—depend essentially on our interaction with others, even on our *not* being left alone, but drawn into collective life.)

In conclusion, to close the circle, I suggest that one central presupposition of the existence of freedom, as I have analysed it, is that the individual is respected as a person by others (and respects himself). Indeed, this must logically be so, since, on my analysis, being so respected precisely is (at least in part) what being accorded freedom means. Where such respect is lacking, a person's freedom will be endangered: his autonomy will be reduced, his privacy invaded and his self-development stunted.

CHAPTER 19

The Doctrines

What relations hold between the remaining unit-ideas of individualism that we have distinguished? In seeking to answer this question, we may be brief, since the answer is already implicit in our discussion of the doctrines of individualism in Part Two.

The first point to notice is that the notion of the abstract individual is central to many versions of most of these doctrines. It runs like a connecting thread through the various forms of political individualism, from Locke to the present day, which, as we have suggested, all presuppose a picture of civil society, whose members are 'independent centres of consciousness' and have given, non-context-dependent interests, wants, motives, purposes, needs, etc. The picture is one of *societas* rather than *communitas*, of partnership rather than corporate unity, of *Gesellschaft* or association rather than *Gemeinschaft* or community. The authority of government rests on the citizens' independently-given consent, represents individual interests, and protects their freedom or rights to pursue their interests. Thus for Locke, man in the state of nature is 'free, . . . absolute lord of his own person and possessions, equal to the greatest and subject to nobody': such a man comes 'to join in society with others' for 'the mutual preservation of their lives, liberties and estates, which I call by the general name, property'.[1] As

[1] Locke, *The Second Treatise of Civil Government*, Ch. IX, Sec. 123 p. 62.

Macpherson has truly said, the 'core of Locke's individualism is the assertion that every man is naturally the sole proprietor of his own person and capacities—the absolute proprietor in that he owes nothing to society for them—and especially the absolute proprietor of his capacity to labour'.[2] The idea of the independent, rational citizen is a central presupposition of classical liberal democratic theory, above all in its eighteenth and nineteenth century forms, whether contractarian or utilitarian—both of which are at present undergoing a revival, as in the work of John Rawls[3] and, e.g., Anthony Downs[4] respectively.

The abstract individual is no less a presupposition of economic individualism, in the form of 'economic man'—rationally seeking to maximize utility—who is still at the centre of orthodox economic theory. Of this conception of man there has never perhaps been a sharper critic than Thorstein Veblen: he saw it as that of

a lightning calculator of pleasures and pains, who oscillates like a homogeneous globule of desire of happiness under the impulse of stimuli that shift him about the area, but leave him intact. He has neither antecedent nor consequent. He is an isolated definitive human datum, in stable equilibrium except for the buffets of the impinging forces that displace him in one direction or another. Self-imposed in elemental space, he spins symmetrically about his own spiritual axis until the parallelogram of forces bears down

[2] Macpherson, *The Political Theory of Possessive Individualism; Hobbes to Locke*, p. 260.

[3] *See* J. Rawls, *A Theory of Justice*, Oxford, 1972. Interestingly, Rawls claims that his rational men, deciding on the principles of justice behind a 'veil of ignorance', are unaware of their future tastes and desires, and that these are therefore not pre-determined by his theory. But, in the present writer's opinion, it can fairly easily be shown that Rawlsian men have a certain fixed range of modern liberal beliefs and wants built into them.

[4] *See* A. Downs, *An Economic Theory of Democracy*, New York, 1957.

upon him, whereupon he follows the line of the resultant. When the force of the impact is spent he comes to rest, a self-contained glubule of desire as before.[5]

Neither religious nor ethical individualism, however, pre-supposes an abstract individual. The religious believer and the sovereign chooser of values that they respectively postulate are real, concrete, historically and socially located persons. Exponents of the essentially modern doctrine of ethical individualism, for example, such as Nietzsche, Weber and Sartre, were certainly conscious of historical and social influences on the individual mind. The ethical egoist, however, was one historically important and influential type of abstract individual, especially in the seventeenth and eighteenth centuries. The individual of epistemological individualism is, by definition, abstract, since this doctrine precludes consideration of the impact of social, cultural and linguistic factors on the individual's mind and experience: thus Descartes, Kant and the British empiricists all begin from the 'individual', abstracted (unsuccessfully, of course) from his social context. The 'social construction of reality' and the socio-historical determination of experience are ideas which their theories necessarily exclude. (It is really only with Hegel that they first appear.) Lastly, if my arguments concerning methodological individualism are correct, then, if the allegedly explanatory 'individuals' are abstract, the doctrine is interesting but highly implausible; while if they are not, it is uninteresting, since social factors have already been built into them.

Turning next to political individualism, there are, it will be obvious, close conceptual links between it and economic individualism. As suggested above, they both presuppose an

[5] M. Lerner (ed.), *The Portable Veblen*, New York, 1948, pp. 232–3, cited in E. K. Hunt and Jesse G. Schwartz (eds.), *A Critique of Economic Theory* (Penguin Education), London, 1972, p. 11.

abstract individual—and, most often, the *same* abstract individual—'rational' and calculating, utility-maximizing and non-altruistic. As Beer writes of the nineteenth-century Liberals, in 'their politics, as in their economics, the source of action was (or ought to be) the rational, independent individual'.[6] Moreover, in many cases, their mode of argument is identical, reasoning deductively from rational, abstract men with determinate but conflicting wants: thus the early Utilitarians, in particular, applied their methods equally to economics and to politics (though John Stuart Mill was to argue that their methods were applicable to the former but not to the latter).[7] And finally, the interests which the political individualist sees the government as representing, protecting and promoting are, from Locke to Hayek, characteristically individual economic interests.

Neither political nor economic individualism is logically or conceptually tied to religious, ethical or epistemological individualism; but there is a clear affinity, especially in the case of economic individualism, with the doctrine of methodological individualism. Seeing political institutions and activities and economic processes as the outcome of the given wants of rational individuals in interaction goes most naturally with the view that the latter exclusively explain the former (together with a systematic blindness to the ways in which individuals' wants, motives, beliefs and purposes are shaped and influenced by institutions and cultures). Thus it is not surprising that Hayek, for example, sees it as a mistake to suppose that the aim

[6] Beer, *Modern British Politics*, p. 34.
[7] *See* J. S. Mill, *A System of Logic*, 10th ed., London, 1879, Vol. II, Bk. VI, Ch. IX. *See* esp. p. 502: '. . . there can be no separate Science of Government; that being the fact which, of all others, is most mixed up, both as cause and effect, with the qualities of the particular people or of the particular age. All questions respecting the tendencies of forms of government must stand part of the general Science of Society, not of any separate branch of it.'

of the social sciences is to explain 'conscious action' (this—if it can be done at all—being the task of psychology):

For the social sciences the types of individual conscious action are data and all they have to do with regard to these data is to arrange them in such orderly fashion that they can be effectively used for their task. The problems which they try to answer arise only in so far as the conscious action of many men produce undesigned results, in so far as regularities are observed which are not the result of anybody's design.[8]

Next, we can observe that the links between religious and ethical individualism are extremely close. Indeed, the distinction between them is, from a religious point of view, artificial. In other words, the very distinction between religious and moral values is (on certain all-embracing views of religion) itself a non-religious distinction, so that from such a religious perspective, what we have called ethical individualism may be seen as a (modern) variant of religious individualism. And, even from a secular perspective, the distinction is hardly clearcut: where, after all, does religion end and morality begin? Recall that Weber, in expounding what we have called his ethical individualism, wrote that 'the individual has to decide which is God for him, and which is the devil'.[9] (And he quotes James Mill—of all people—to the effect that 'If one proceeds from pure experience, one arrives at polytheism').[10] On the other hand, an extreme ethical individualist, such as the early Sartre, will argue that the very belief in a God is a form of bad faith. Since God does not exist, the individual is 'without excuse': we are no longer 'provided with any values or commands that could legitimize our behaviour'.[11]

[8] Hayek, *The Counter-Revolution of Science*, pp. 37–8.
[9] 'Politics as a Vocation' in Gerth and Mills, *From Max Weber*, p. 148.
[10] *Ibid.*, p. 147.   [11] Sartre, *Existentialism and Humanism*, pp. 33–4.

Religious and ethical individualism are not conceptually or logically related to epistemological and methodological individualism (though Hume traced morality and knowledge alike to 'perceptions in the mind'), but these last two doctrines have a certain structural similarity with one another. Epistemological individualism, above all in its empiricist form, shares with methodological individualism an atomistic or reductionist tendency: the former seeking to reconstruct knowledge out of its simplest elements, the latter claiming that social phenomena can only be explained by breaking them down into their simplest elements, namely individuals. (And, unfortunately, in both cases, the putative atoms, the allegedly simplest elements, are in fact irreducibly pre-determined by the *Gestalt* of which they form part, and indeed their features cannot be identified without reference to it.)

In conclusion, it is interesting to note that many of the doctrines of individualism appeal to and propose ways of realizing what we have called the 'core values' of individualism. Political individualism incorporates a core element of democratic equality and thus equal respect for persons (hence, for instance men's equality in the state of nature or in voting rights); it also postulates autonomy (especially in the giving of consent and in the pursuit of interests). But perhaps the paramount value this doctrine seeks to advance is that of preserving private, 'negative' liberty—though some have also defended it, or parts of it, as means to self-realization. Economic individualism is, equally, seen by its proponents as uniquely consonant with individualist values. The very impersonality of the market, according to its defenders, makes for a kind of equality before its laws: it favours only those who are deservedly successful through effort or skill, and those blessed, at random and thus indiscriminately, by good luck. Economic individualists also seek to maximize autonomy: hence Hayek's preference for the 'hard discipline of the market' on the grounds that it still leaves the individual 'some choice', as opposed to a system of planning, which 'leaves him none'.[12] Being left alone to exercise that choice—keeping valued economic activities *private*—is, of course, the central value they seek to realize, but often on the further ground that such economic freedom will best promote self-development. As the passage we quoted from H. M. Robertson correctly observed, economic individualism

... seeks to realize social progress through the individual by allowing him all the scope for his free self-development which is possible. It believes that for this two institutions are necessary: economic freedom (that is, freedom of enterprise) and private property. It believes that different individuals have different aptitudes and that each should be allowed to develop them in competition with others to the best of his ability.[13]

The religious individualist likewise appeals to individualist values. He believes in the spiritual equality of all believers and he sees the individual believer as aiming at spiritual self-perfection. He holds that the individual's achievement of that state and his relationship with God are the result of autonomous choice, effort and spiritual self-examination: no other human being or human institution is responsible, and he cannot rely on external and collective intermediaries to achieve salvation for him. As for privacy, this is given effect, in the case of religious individualism, by toleration: the meaning of religious toleration is precisely the granting of a private space for the unhindered performance of highly, perhaps supremely, valued religious activity. Finally, ethical individualism, as we have suggested, can be seen as the philosophical consequence of taking the idea of autonomy to a logical extreme. If the very criteria of moral judgement, and even of what is to count as a

[12] Hayek, *Individualism and Economic Order*, p. 24.
[13] Roberston, *Aspects of the Rise of Economic Individualism*, p. 34.

moral judgement, are up for individual choice, then the individual who makes such choices is, in one sense, exercising autonomy in the most basic possible way—though it is interesting that many of those who are tempted by this doctrine tend to see that autonomy as a burden to be accepted rather than as a condition to be welcomed.

We have seen, then, that there are a number of interrelations between the various individualist doctrines we have identified, and that some of them appeal to the core values of individualism. But does adherence to those values require us to accept the doctrines? It is to this question that the next, and final, chapter is devoted.

CHAPTER 20

Taking Equality and Liberty Seriously

relation
bet 18 & 19

What does a commitment to equality and liberty—to respecting persons, to maintaining and enhancing their autonomy, privacy and self-development—imply?

It does not, to begin with, imply the adoption of what we have called the abstract conception of the individual. It is, of course, true that any way of conceiving individuals requires abstraction, since it involves the use of concepts. However, the abstract conception presents the individual as consisting merely in a certain set of invariant psychological characteristics and tendencies—as having certain sorts of wants and purposes, as acting on certain sorts of motives, as having certain interests. Conceiving of an individual as a *person*, by contrast, presents him as the source of (yet to be discovered) intentions and purposes, decisions and choices, as capable of engaging in and valuing certain (yet to be discovered) activities and involvements, and as capable of (yet to be discovered) forms of self-development. The former view defines the individual as a human being with certain psychological features, which determine his behaviour; the latter defines a person as a human being with certain *capacities*, the degree and form of whose realization is left open for investigation. The abstract individual is the product of an (unacceptable) theory; the concept of a person is a way of seeing individuals, whose content is to be determined by observing them. Thus, seeing them *as* persons requires us to abstract *from* socially-given abstractions, namely definitions, typifications, categories or labels, which typecast them and thereby limit the possibilities of our understanding them. Seeing them as persons requires us precisely to regard them not *merely* as the bearers of certain titles, the players of certain roles or the occupiers of certain social positions, or as the means to given ends, but as concrete persons who—for one reason or another, in one fashion or another—bear those titles, play those roles, occupy those social positions, or serve those ends. It does not, however, require us to see them as having fixed and universal human attributes—given wants, purposes, interests, needs—that have their source and can be characterized independently of their social contexts. Quite the contrary: we owe each of them what Bernard Williams calls 'an effort at identification', so that 'he should not be regarded as the surface to which a certain label can be applied, but one should try to see the world (including the label) from his point of view.'[1] And that point of view will, of course, be socially determinate and located, and only characterizable in socially specific terms.

Nor does a commitment to equality and liberty, as we have analysed them, logically imply the acceptance of individualist political, economic or religious doctrines. Such a commitment is entirely compatible with the denial of the theories of governmental legitimacy, political representation and the purposes of government, which we have collectively labelled political individualism. It is likewise compatible with the denial of economic individualism: a believer in socialist planning is—*pace* Hayek—not necessarily (though he may be in fact) an enemy of human dignity, and of the values of autonomy, privacy and self-development. Nor, similarly, is a non-individualist or corporatist view of religion *eo ipso* a denial of the core values of individualism: one can adhere to the latter while accepting the former.

[1] Williams, 'The Idea of Equality', p. 117.

Again, there is no inherent logical connection between equality and liberty, as we have analysed them, on the one hand, and individualist philosophical doctrines concerning the source and grounds of morality and of knowledge, on the other. A commitment to the component values of the former carries no implications that one must in consequence accept an individualist ethics or epistemology. And the same goes for methodological individualism. Despite what many adherents of that doctrine assert, there appears to be no reason why one may not deny its exclusivist claim (i.e. that only features or actions of individuals are explanatory) while remaining a firm believer in the supreme importance of respecting persons, and valuing their autonomy, their privacy and their self-development.

So far, I have sought to establish the negative thesis that a commitment to the central values of individualism does not require us to adopt any of the remaining ideas and doctrines distinguished in the second Part of this book. I now wish to advance the positive and bolder thesis that, if we are to take those values seriously today, we must explicitly reject a number of these further ideas and doctrines, and adopt others instead. Proving this thesis would be a considerable task, and even to support it adequately would require far more space than is at my disposal. All I can hope to do here is to advance a number of considerations that argue in its favour.

In the first place, I have already suggested that the principle of respect for persons requires, among other things, that we regard and act towards individuals in their concrete specificity, that we take full account of their specific aims and purposes and of their own definitions of their (social) situations. And I have also argued that this means in practice, among other things, that we see them as the (actually or potentially) autonomous sources of decisions and choices, as engaging in activities and involvements which they value highly and which require protection from public interference, and as capable of realizing certain potentialities, which will take a distinctive form in each specific individual's case. Respecting them as *persons*, in these ways, involves the kind of understanding of both their social and their individual aspects which the abstract view of them precludes. For, on the one hand, such respect requires us to take account of them as social selves—moulded and constituted by their societies—whose achievement of, and potential for, autonomy, whose valued activities and involvements and whose potentialities are, in large part, socially determined and specific to their particular social contexts. On the other hand, it requires us to see each of them as an actually or potentially autonomous centre of choice (rather than a bundle composed of a certain range of wants, motives, purposes, interests, etc.), able to choose between, and on occasion transcend, socially-given activities and involvements, and to develop his or her respective potentialities in the available forms sanctioned by the culture—which is both a structural constraint and a determinant of individuality.

Now, there is no doubt that historically, the abstract conception of the individual represented a major moral advance. It was a decisive step in the direction of a universalist ethics when human beings first came to be regarded as the possessors of certain rights and claims, simply in virtue of being human. But on the other hand, the very abstractness of this view also constituted a serious limitation. Seeing real, actual individuals as so many representatives of the genus *man* involved singling out a particular set of characteristics—particular motives, interests, needs, etc.—as distinctively human; and this was, at the same time, a way of seeing society and social relations, in a particular way. But every way of seeing is also a way of not seeing; and in this case a view of man as essentially property-owning or self-interested or 'rational' or concerned to maximize his utility amounts to the ideological legitimation of a particular view of society and social relations—and the implicit delegitimation of others. Marx put this point with considerable clarity and force in his critique of Bentham. The principle of utility, he wrote,

was no discovery of Bentham. He simply reproduced in his dull way what Helvétius and other Frenchmen had said with esprit in the eighteenth century. [How *could* Marx call Bentham's style dull?]. To know what is useful for a dog, one must study dog-nature. This nature itself is not to be deduced from the principle of utility. Applying this to man, he that would criticize all human acts, movements, relations, etc., by the principle of utility, must first deal with human nature in general, and then with human nature as modified in each historical epoch. Bentham makes short work of it. With the dryest naïveté he takes the modern shopkeeper, especially the English shopkeeper, as the normal man. Whatever is useful to this queer normal man, and to his world, is absolutely useful. This yard-measure, then, he applies to past, present and future. The Christian religion, *e.g.*, is 'useful', because it forbids in the name of religion the same faults that the penal code condemns in the name of the law. . . . Had I the courage of my friend Heinrich Heine, I should call Mr. Jeremy a genius in the way of bourgeois stupidity.[2]

Precisely what the abstract view of the individual precludes is an appreciation of the ways in which 'human nature' is 'modified in each historical epoch'. More fundamentally, it is at odds with what Dumont calls the 'sociological apperception'—the 'apperception of the social nature of man', which 'opposes man as a social being' to 'the self-sufficient individual' and which 'considers each man no longer as a particular incarnation of abstract humanity, but as a more or less autonomous point of emergence of a particular collective humanity, of a *society*'.[3] This was exactly Marx's thought when he wrote that '*man* is not an abstract being squatting outside the world.

[2] Marx, *Capital*, Vol. I, Ch. XXIV, Sec. 5, pp. 609–10, fn. 2.
[3] Dumont, *Homo Hierarchicus*, p. 5.

He is *the human world*, the state, society'.[4] In contrast to the individualist picture of individuals as like onions which, once their outer, culturally-relative skins are peeled off, are 'much the same in all times and places',[5] the sociological apperception reveals society as irreducibly constitutive of or built into the individual in crucial and profound ways. His distinctively human qualities, even his very capacity (and of course opportunities) to achieve autonomy and self-development are in large measure socially determined. To quote Dumont once more:

Think . . . of the child, slowly brought to humanity by upbringing in the family, by the apprenticeship of language and moral judgement, by the education which makes him share in the common patrimony—including, in our society, elements which were unknown to the whole of mankind less than a century ago. Where would be the humanity of this man, where his understanding, without the training or taming, properly speaking a creation, which every society imparts to its members, by whatever actual agency?[6]

The abstract conception of the individual, in other words, directly contradicts all the accumulated lessons of sociology and social anthropology and of social psychology. As George H. Mead—to cite a final, and incisive, exponent of the sociological apperception—acutely observed, 'a person is a personality because he belongs to a community, because he takes over the institutions of that community into his own conduct'.[7] The individual self is not merely essentially social in its formation and nature; its very individuality is to be seen as formed of

[4] Marx, *Early Writings*, p. 43.
[5] Hume, *Essays Moral and Political*, Vol. II, p. 68.
[6] Dumont, *op. cit.*, p. 5.
[7] From *Mind, Self and Society*, reprinted in *The Social Psychology of George Herbert Mead*, edited with an introduction by Anselm Strauss (Phoenix Books), Chicago, 1956, p. 239.

L

social elements. The self, as Mead put it, 'reaches its full development by organizing these individual attitudes of others
into the organized social or group attitudes, and by thus becoming an individual reflection of the general systematic pattern of
social or group behaviour in which it and the others are all
involved.' However,

The fact that all selves are constituted by or in terms of the social
process, and are individual reflections of it—or rather of this organized behaviour pattern which it exhibits, and which they prehend in
their respective structures—is not in the least incompatible with, or
destructive of, the fact that every individual self has its own peculiar
individuality, its own unique pattern; because each individual self
within that process, while it reflects in its organized structure the
behaviour pattern of that process as a whole, does so from its own
particular and unique standpoint within that process, and thus
reflects in its organized structure a different aspect or perspective of
this whole social behaviour pattern from that which is reflected in
the organized structure of any other individual self within that
process (just as every monad in the Leibnizian universe mirrors that
universe from a different point of view, and thus mirrors a different
aspect or perspective of that universe).[8]

I have argued that the abstract conception of the individual
is doubly inadequate: first, because it in fact forms the basis for
a particular ideological view of a certain sort of society and its
social relations; and second, because it represents a primitive
and a- or pre-sociological view of the nature of the individual.
But I have also suggested that this way of conceiving the individual was historically progressive. It was a crucial weapon in the
breaking down of traditional privileges and hierarchies, in the
dissolution of separate and incommensurable social orders and
ranks, and in the establishing of universal human claims in the
form of legal rights. The formal legal framework of modern

    [8] *Ibid.*, pp. 235, 247–8.

democratic societies is the guardian of the abstract individual. It provides for formal equality (before the law) and formal freedom (from illegal or arbitrary treatment). These are crucial and indispensable gains but, if we are to take equality and liberty seriously, they must be transcended. And that can only be achieved on the basis of a view of un-abstracted individuals in their concrete, social specificity, who, in virtue of being *persons*, all require to be treated and to live in a social order which treats them as possessing dignity, as capable of exercising and increasing their autonomy, of engaging in valued activities within a private space, and of developing their several potentialities.

Political and economic individualism are similarly to be seen as having been historically progressive but as currently requiring to be transcended, though in different ways.

Political individualism, as I have suggested, played a major historical role in the development of the liberal-democratic State—and the (Whig) history of the progressive influence of these ideas has been told in countless histories of political thought. The individualist view of consent had an inherently anti-authoritarian thrust (though it could itself be used to justify other forms of authoritarianism, as with the Jacobins); the individualist theory of representation, as we have seen, played a part in the breaking down of political inequalities and the establishing of universal suffrage and a uniform franchise; while the individualist theory of the purposes of government was central to the growth of limited government, constitutional safeguards and the protection of individual rights. But all these doctrines rest on a view of the individual, and thus of society and social relations, which is subject to the inadequacies we have specified above. Moreover, the specific doctrines of political individualism present a picture of politics which anyone concerned to take equality and liberty seriously can no longer find satisfactory. As an account of the actual practice of politics in modern liberal democratic societies, it is naïve and irrelevant: it is hardly illuminating to see the practice of contemporary American or British or French politics in terms of individually given consent, the representation of individual interests, and the protection of all the citizens' private interests. On the other hand, it fares no better as an account of a possible and desirable form of politics that would maximize equality and liberty in advanced industrial societies. Which is not to say that such a politics would dispense with the need for consent, representation and the protection of interests. But it would need to conceptualize these in a much more complex way, and take full account of the many degrees and modes of consent (and the acute problem of distinguishing true from false consensus), of different ways of implementing democracy than through legislative 'representatives' and different ways of conceiving 'representation' (e.g. of different social roles, or activities, or aspects of the individual), and finally of the need for such a democratic and representative government to take an ever more active role in shaping and controlling the natural and social environment if equality and liberty are to be enhanced.

The case for the historical progressiveness of economic individualism—and of the economic system it celebrated—is no less familiar, and was indeed powerfully advanced by Marx himself. The case for its contemporary irrelevance and regressiveness is equally familiar—and convincing, despite the warnings of Hayek, Friedman and the Chicago school against the dangers of 'interventionist chaos' and wholesale social engineering. Quite apart from the ever-growing gap between the economic individualist model and the corporate neo-capitalist reality, the prescriptions of economic individualism, while appealing to the values of equality and liberty, in fact amount to their denial. (Consider, for example, Hayek's advocacy of 'natural' inequality, the role of accident and an 'independent' class, and his extremely narrow and tendentious definition of liberty, which would preclude calling violations of liberty most of the characteristic evils of capitalism). Whatever the threats to equality and liberty that are posed by the State's control over production and distribution—and whatever the threats to liberty involved in taking equality seriously—it is quite unwarranted to oppose socialist planning and redistribution in the name of those values. The urgent task is rather to find ways of reconciling the former with the latter.

As for the relation between a serious commitment to equality and liberty, on the one hand, and religious individualism, on the other, it is impossible to say anything useful in so short a space. Suffice it here to say that there are at least two broad views of religion, which carry opposite implications in this connection (of which the present writer takes the second). On the one hand, one may regard religious faith and practice as entirely compatible with fully autonomous human activity and self-development, and perhaps even as an (or the) essential component of them; or one may see religion as ultimately a set of illusions, however deep and complex and however rich in incidental wisdom, which, for that reason, is not compatible with the full development by individuals of their consciousness of themselves and their situation, and of their human powers. On the first view, religion is an aspect of the human condition which men need not, or cannot, or perhaps should not seek to transcend; on the second, one will concur with Marx's observation that the 'abolition of religion as the *illusory* happiness of men, is a demand for their *real* happiness. The call to abandon their illusions about their condition is a *call to abandon a condition which requires illusions*'.[9]

Are equality and liberty, as we have analysed them, ultimately compatible with ethical individualism? On the face of

[9] Marx, *Contribution to the Critique of Hegel's Philosophy of Right: Introduction*, in *Early Writings*, p. 44.

it, the answer to this question might appear to be 'yes', since, as we have seen, ethical individualism can be seen as an extreme form of moral autonomy. However, there is an important difference between autonomy, as we have analysed it—as self-determined deciding and choosing on the basis of consciousness of one's self and one's situation—and the extreme and intransigent moral pluralism implicit in ethical individualism. (Indeed, it is arguable that ethical individualism, in proposing a limit to the giving of reasons in moral argument, so that ultimately the individual performs an *acte gratuit* of reasonless 'commitment', thereby denies the possibility of realizing autonomy at all—since, on my account, autonomy is intimately connected with consciousness and 'critical reflection', which themselves involve an appeal to rationality. If moral choice is ultimately non-rational, how can its exercise be autonomous? But to this it may be countered: if moral judgement is ultimately rational, how can it be a matter of choice?) Moreover, if the core values of individualism which jointly constitute the ideals of equality and liberty are more than merely formal, if, in other words, they have a determinate moral *content*, then adhering to them will be strictly incompatible with adhering to the doctrine of ethical individualism. This emerges especially clearly in the case of the value of self-development. If, as I have argued, the notion of self-development incorporates an irreducible teleological component, a belief in the existence of some determinate range of characteristic human excellences and the denial that what these consist in (and preclude) is open to irresolvable dispute, then taking this central value of individualism seriously will require one to reject the extreme moral relativism or pluralism inherent in the doctrine of ethical individualism.

There is, as far as I can see, no apparent connection between a commitment to the values of individualism and either the acceptance or rejection of epistemological individualism, but the same is not true of methodological individualism. Taking equality and liberty seriously implies seeking to ascertain the conditions under which they can be realized, maintained and increased. It should be very clear from our all too brief discussion of these ideals that these conditions are primarily social and political. Thus, for example, one will need to look very closely at the structural determinants of status ranking if one is concerned to increase equality, or at the deeper influences (e.g. through language and perception)[10] of the agencies of socialization, if one is concerned to maximize autonomy and self-development throughout all sections of society. In this way, sociological and social psychological inquiry is an essential prerequisite of egalitarian and libertarian social change. Hence, a methodology which (in a non-trivial form) simply precludes one from examining the deeper structural and institutional forces which constitute the central obstacles to such change must clearly be rejected as not merely theoretically narrow, but as socially and politically regressive.

It was suggested in the previous chapter that most of the individualist doctrines we have considered appeal to the core values of individualism. In this chapter I have argued that it is not merely possible to hold to these values while rejecting the doctrines, but that taking the values seriously requires us to abandon most of the doctrines. I have, needless to say, been unable to prove that latter claim here. Still less have I here proved what I take to be its most important corollary, implicit in the arguments advanced above—that the only way to realize the values of individualism is through a humane form of socialism.

[10] See, e.g., the work of Basil Bernstein, as collected in B. Bernstein, Class, Codes and Control. Volume I: Theoretical Studies towards a Sociology of Language, London, 1971.

Afterword

The third Part of this book provides a sort of conceptual map of certain relations between what emerged out of the preceding analysis as the core values of individualism. That map presents equality in terms of liberty, and both liberty and equality in terms of what are claimed to be the more basic unit-ideas of respect for persons, autonomy, privacy and self-development.

About that map three concluding remarks may be in order. First, it is not (and could not be) value-neutral: it is constructed from within a particular moral and political perspective. Second, it is, precisely, *constructed*, though not arbitrarily so. It is a way—hopefully a rationally persuasive way—of organizing the conceptual field in question. And at this point the analogy of the map begins to break down. For the relation of representation to what is represented differs from that in cartography. The second is not independent of the first: the map itself serves to organize and structure the conceptual field. My claim is that the map sketched above both arises out of the history of the concepts and provides a consistent and valuable framework for moral and political discourse. But, in the third place, it is a map which is radically incomplete. In particular, it leaves out of account the many possible conflicts between these ideas; and it focuses on liberty and equality, but ignores the crucial third term of fraternity, or community. In mitigation, I plead limitation of space, and, as regards the second lacuna, the title of the book itself. For, if the analysis it offers is correct, it is liberty and equality which are the cardinal ideals of individualism.

Bibliography

Arendt, H., *The Human Condition*, Garden City, 1959.

Arieli, Y., *Individualism and Nationalism in American Ideology*, Cambridge, Mass., 1964.

Beer, S. H., *Modern British Politics*, London, 1965.

Berlin, Sir I., *Four Essays on Liberty*, Oxford, 1969.

Burckhardt, G., *Was ist Individualismus?*, Leipzig, 1913.

Burckhardt, J., *The Civilization of the Renaissance in Italy* (1860) tr. by S. G. C. Middlemore, London, 1955.

Cumming, R. D., *Human Nature and History*, Chicago and London, 1969, 2 Vols: Vol 2, Part IV: 'Individualism'.

Dicey, A. V., *Law and Public Opinion in England* (1905), London, 1962.

Dietzel, H., 'Individualismus', *Handwörterbuch der Staatswissenschaften*, 4th rev. ed., Jena, 1923, Vol V, pp. 408–24.

Downie, R. S. and Telfer, E., *Respect for Persons*, London, 1969.

Dray, W. H., 'Holism and Individualism in History and Social Science' in P. Edwards (ed.), *The Encyclopaedia of Philosophy*, New York, 1967. (For bibliography on this subject, see n. 11, pp. 113–14 of the present work).

Dumont, L., 'The Modern Conception of the Individual: notes on its genesis and that of concomitant institutions', *Contributions to Indian Sociology* VIII (1965), pp. 13–61.

  Homo Hierarchicus: The Caste System and its Implications, tr. by Mark Sainsbury, London, 1970, Introduction.

  'Religion, Politics and Society in the Individualistic Universe' (The Henry Myers Lecture 1970) in *Proceedings of Royal Anthropological Institute*, 1970, pp. 31–41.

M

Durkheim, É., 'Individualism and the Intellectuals' (1898), tr. by S. and J. Lukes, *Political Studies*, XVII (1969), pp. 19–30.

Gierke, O., *Das deutsche Genossenschaft*, Berlin, 1913, IV, 14–18, translated as *Natural Law and the Theory of Society, 1500–1800*, by E. Barker, Cambridge, 1934, 2 Vols, and Boston, 1957, 1 Vol.

Ginsberg, M., 'The Individual and Society' in *On the Diversity of Morals*, London, 1956.

Halévy, É., *The Growth of Philosophical Radicalism* (1901–4), tr. by M. Morris, new ed., London, 1934.

Hayek, F. A., *Individualism and Economic Order*, London, 1949.

The Constitution of Liberty, Chicago, 1960.

Hobhouse, L. T., *Liberalism* (1911) (Galaxy Book), New York, 1964.

Hofstadter, R., *Social Darwinism in American Thought*, New York, 1959.

Hospers, J., *Libertarianism: A Political Philosophy for Tomorrow*, Los Angeles, 1971.

Koebner, R., 'Zur Begriffsbildung der Kulturgeschichte: II: Zur Geschichte des Begriffs "Individualismus"' (Jacob Burckhardt, Wilhelm von Humboldt und die französische Soziologie)', *Historische Zeitschrift*, CXLIX (1934), pp. 253–93.

Koehler, F., *Wesen und Bedeutung des Individualismus, Eine Studie*, München, 1922.

Lindsay, A. D., 'Individualism', *Encyclopedia of the Social Sciences*, New York, 1930–33, Vol. VII, pp. 674–80.

MacIntyre, A., *A Short History of Ethics*, London, 1967.

Macpherson, C. B., *The Political Theory of Possessive Individualism: Hobbes to Locke*, Oxford, 1962.

McTaggart, J. McT. E., 'The Individualism of Value' in *Philosophical Studies*, London, 1934.

Marion, H., 'Individualisme' in *La Grande Encyclopédie* (Paris, n.d.), Vol. XX.

Mauss, M., 'Une Catégorie de l'esprit humain: la notion de personne, celle de "moi", un plan du travail', *Journal of the Royal Anthropological Institute*, LXVIII (1938), pp. 263–81, republished in M. Mauss, *Sociologie et anthropologie*, intro. by C. Lévi-Strauss, Paris, 1950, 3rd ed., 1966, Pt. V.

Moulin, L., 'On the Evolution of the Meaning of the Word "Individualism"', *International Social Science Bulletin*, VII (1955), pp. 181–5.

Palmer, R. R., 'Man and Citizen: Applications of Individualism in the French Revolution', *Essays in Political Theory presented to G. H. Sabine*, Ithaca, N.Y., 1948.

Popper, Sir K., *The Open Society and Its Enemies*, London, 1945 (4th ed., 1962), 2 Vols.

The Poverty of Historicism, London, 1957.

Rawls, J., *A Theory of Justice*, Oxford, 1972.

Riesman, D., *Individualism Reconsidered*, Glencoe, Ill., 1954, abridged ed. (Anchor Books), Garden City, n.d.

Robertson, H. M., *Aspects of the Rise of Economic Individualism*, Cambridge, 1933.

Sartre, J. P., *Existentialism and Humanism*, tr. by P. Mairet, London, 1948.

Schatz, A., *L'Individualisme économique et sociale*, Paris, 1907.

Simmel, G., *The Sociology of George Simmel*, tr. and ed. with introd. by K. H. Wolff, Glencoe, Ill., 1950, pp. 58–84.

Swart, K. W., ' "Individualism" in the Mid-Nineteenth Century (1826–60)', *Journal of the History of Ideas*, XXIII (1962), pp. 77–90.

Tawney, R. H., *Religion and the Rise of Capitalism*, London, 1926, esp. Ch. III, iii.

Tocqueville, A. de, *De la Democratie en Amérique* (1835), Bk. II, Pt. II, Ch. II in *Oeuvres complètes*, ed. J. P. Mayer, Paris, 1951–, I, II, pp. 104–6.

Troeltsch, E., *The Social Teaching of the Christian Churches* (1912), New York, 1931, 2 Vols.

'The Ideas of Natural Law and Humanity in World Politics' (1922) in Gierke, *Natural Law and the Theory of Society, 1500–1800, op. cit.*

Ullmann, W., *The Individual and Society in the Middle Ages*, Baltimore, 1966, London, 1967.

Villey, M., *Leçons d'histoire de la philosophie du droit*, new ed., Paris, 1962.

Watt, I., *The Rise of the Novel: Studies in Defoe, Richardson and*

Fielding, London, 1957, esp. Ch. III: '*Robinson Crusoe*, Individualism and the Novel'.

Weber, M., *The Protestant Ethic and the Spirit of Capitalism* (1904–5), tr. by T. Parsons, London, 1930.

Wolff, R. P., *The Poverty of Liberalism*, Boston, 1968.

In Defence of Anarchism, New York, 1970.

Woodcock, G., *Anarchism*, London, 1963.

Name Index

Subject Index

abstract individual 79, 111, 123; history of concept 73–8; and equality of opportunity 127; and doctrines of individualism 138–40; vs. 'persons' 146–7; value of concept 149, 152; its inadequacy 150–2
anarchism 48, 72 n. 15
anarchy 8, 9, 10, 26
anomie 15, 57
aristocratic thought 13, 14, 76
art, artists 19, 25, 68, 69; for Marx 71
association 10, 11, 138
atomism: in USA 30; Utilitarian 48; psychological 108; logical 109
atomization 8, 10, 33, 40
Austrian school (of political economy) *see* economic theories
authority 11, 24, 50, 138; in Diderot's *Encyclopedia* 81
Autobiography (Mill) 69
autonomy of the individual ix, 12, 52–8; in Renaissance thought 24, 53–4; and religion 52–3; and liberty 55–6; in modern society 56–7; and determinism 57–8; and doctrines of individualism 135, 136, 143, 144, 156

Benthamism 35, 38–9, 41
Bolshevism 42
Boston Quarterly Review 27
bourgeoisie 11, 84–5
Brook Farm 29

Calvinism 40, 95–6
capitalism 10, 32, 40; and Saint-Simonism 6; and individualism in USA 26, 92, 93; and individualist values 124, 154, 155
Catholicism 4, 34, 95
censorship 136
Chicago school (of political economy) *see* economic theories
choice: existentialist 105; moral 105–6, 144–5, 156; and autonomy 127, 128, 129, 131, 144–5; for Mill 135; for Berlin 136; for Hayek 143–4; in definition of 'person' 149
Christianity ix, 40, 96, 97, 98; and dignity of man 45–6, 126, 131; and autonomy 52–3. *See also* religion
'Civil Disobedience' (Thoreau) 82
Civilization in the Renaissance in Italy (Burckhardt) 23
class 85, 86–7, 121, 155

Epicureanism 40, 60

epistemological individualism 107–109; and other doctrines of individualism 140, 141, 143; and implications of commitment to liberty and equality 148, 156

equality 125–7; of opportunity 26, 30, 37, 126–7; and political individualism 143, 153–4; implications of commitment to 146–53; and economic individualism 154–5; and doctrines of individualism 155–7

esprit particulier 4

ethical individualism 99–106; vs. ethical egoism 100–1; and moral relativism 101–2, 156; and existentialism 104–6; and religion 101, 102–5, 142; and other doctrines of individualism 140, 141, 143, 144; and implications of commitment to liberty and equality 148, 155–6

Ethics (Spinoza) 54

evolutionsim 27, 28, 30, 35

existentialism 104–6

explanation 118–22

Fascism 42, 48, 66 n. 14, 87

France: sense of 'individualism' in 3–16, 78

freedom: for Spinoza 54, 58; for Kant 55; for Berlin 55–6, 62, 64, 128; 'positive' 55–6; 'negative' 62–4, 128, 143; and autonomy 54–6, 127–8, 131, 136; and privacy 62–4, 127, 129, 131; existentialist 105; analysis of 125, 127–30; and self-development 127, 129–31; implications of commitment to 146–53; and political individualism 153–4; and economic individualism 154–5

and doctrines of individualism 155–7

free enterprise 88–91, 144; in USA 27, 29, 30

Free Life, The 38

French Revolution 3, 14

German historical school (of political economy) *see* economic theories

Germany 3; sense of 'individualism' in 17, 22, 67, 78

Gospels, the 45

Great Chain of Being 47–8

Greeks 60

groups in society *see* intermediary groups

historical necessity 11, 25

historians 40–2

Homme machine, L' (La Mettrie) 119

humanism 19; in Renaissance 47–48, 53; and existentialism 105; and individualist values 123, 124

hypnotism 129, 136

Idealists 78

individual, the: and society *see* society; abstract conception of *see* abstract individual

individualism: semantic history of 1–42; in France 3–16, 26, 32; in USA 27–31; in Germany 17–25, 32, 33; in England 32–9; quantitative vs. qualitative 17, 67; and German nationalism 20–21; unit ideas of *see* dignity of individuals; autonomy; privacy; self-development; abstract individual; political individualism; economic individualism; religious individualism; ethical individualism; epistemological individual-